Chaos *to* Clarity

A FAMILY-FRIENDLY GUIDE TO DOWNSIZING

By John Greene Jr. & Linda Greene

Copyright © 2025 by John Greene Jr. and Linda Greene.
All rights reserved.

No part of this publication may be reproduced, stored in a retrieval system, or transmitted in any form or by any means, electronic, mechanical, photocopying, recording, scanning, or otherwise, without the prior written permission of the author.

Limit of Liability/Disclaimer of Warranty: While the publisher and author have used their best efforts in preparing this book, they make no representations or warranties with respect to the accuracy or completeness of the contents of this book and specifically disclaim any implied warranties of merchantability or fitness for a particular purpose. No warranty may be created or extended by sales representatives or written sales materials. The advice and strategies contained herein may not be suitable for your situation. You should consult with a professional when appropriate. Neither the publisher nor the author shall be liable for any loss of profit or any other commercial damages, including but not limited to special, incidental, consequential, personal, or other damages.

CHAOS TO CLARITY
A Family-Friendly Guide to Downsizing
By John Greene Jr. and Linda Greene

Library of Congress Control Number: 2025905856

Print ISBN: 978-0-9887770-3-3
Ebook ISBN: 978-0-09887770-1-9
Printed in the United States of America

Subjects: House & Home / Cleaning, Caretaking & Organizing
Family & Relationships / Eldercare

Grey Bird Publishing, LLC Randolph, MA 02368   508-209-5243   www.caringtransitionsssma.com

This book is dedicated to all our senior clients.
Thank you for sharing your wonderful lives.
And all those Hummels.

Disclaimer

This book is based on the experiences and insights gained through our work in senior downsizing. While we operate under the Grey Bird Senior Services LLC, a Caring Transitions® franchise, this book is independent work and does not represent or speak on behalf of C.T. Franchising Systems, Inc. or any other Caring Transitions® franchise location.

Each Caring Transitions® franchise is independently owned and operated. The methods, strategies, and opinions shared in this book reflect our personal experiences in the field and may differ from those of other franchisees. While all Caring Transitions® locations follow a core set of principles and best practices as outlined by the corporate office, the specific approaches, services, and operational methods may vary.

For official information regarding Caring Transitions® services, please refer to the corporate website at www.caringtransitions.com or contact your local franchise directly.

Table of Contents

Introduction   1

SECTION 1 The Heart of Downsizing

- Chapter 1   How Do You Approach Downsizing?   5
- Chapter 2   What's in a House?   12
- Chapter 3   Preparing for the Downsizing Journey   24
- Chapter 4   The Emotional Side of Downsizing   33
- Chapter 5   Family Members We All Have and Love   41

SECTION 2: Blueprint to a New Beginning

- Chapter 6   The Downsizing Process in 4 Phases   51
- Chapter 7   Phase 1: Plan   57
- Chapter 8   Phase 2: Sort & Organize   67
- Chapter 9   Phase 3: Distribute, What Goes Where   87
- Chapter 10   Phase 3: Turning Items Into Cash   98
- Chapter 11   Phase 4: Fix & Final Cleanout   117

SECTION 3: The Final Touches

- Chapter 12   The Tip Jar   123
- Chapter 13   Downsizing To Go - The Move   134
- Chapter 14   Organizing for the Long Haul   138
- Chapter 15   Downsizing Hoarder Houses   144
- Chapter 16   Ways to Save Money in Downsizing   154
- Chapter 17   Murphy's Law of Downsizing   158
- Chapter 18   Putting It All Together   162

Appendix   168

Introduction

"I have too much stuff. I'll never get rid of it."

"Getting old sucks."

"That china cabinet is worth a lot—I paid $4,500 for it!"

We hear things like this almost every day. Downsizing, decluttering, senior move management, or just plain getting rid of stuff - whatever you call it, is tough. But often, we make it harder on ourselves than it needs to be. The good news? Downsizing doesn't have to feel impossible. With the right approach, it can even be (dare we say) enjoyable. This book is here to help.

We've created a method to make downsizing easier, tailored to meet your needs and your family's. Let's start with what we mean by downsizing an estate.

In this book, we cover the downsizing of the physical assets of the estate such as houses, cabins, cottages, sheds, barns, garages, storage units, and sometimes even RVs. Every downsizing effort has two sides: the emotional and the physical.

The Emotional Side

The emotional side is by far the hardest. It varies from person to person, but it's often tied to memories, attachments, and even guilt. We'll explore ways to reduce emotional stress and make this process less overwhelming.

The Physical Side

On the physical side of downsizing, we'll give you a clear process and plan tailored to your situation. Every downsizing project is unique, but they all share common elements. Think of it like underwear—everyone has some! And books, clothes, paperwork, knick-knacks, collectibles, and personal items. The quantities and kinds may differ, but it's always about deciding what to keep, donate, sell, trash, or recycle. In our experience, it's most likely your stuff will bear a strong resemblance to everyone else's. There are outliers (e.g. hoarder houses, mansions, etc.), but most estates have similar items to downsize.

The Bottom Line

Downsizing isn't necessarily hard, but doing it right, and keeping everyone happy, can be tricky. It's not impossible, though. With some planning and foresight, you can make it manageable and even satisfying.

What Are We Downsizing Anyway?

Whether you're Downsizing To Go (a full cleanout) or Downsizing To Stay (decluttering for safety and comfort), this book will guide you step by step.

We'll focus on practical ways to handle the physical assets of an estate—sorting through household contents, buildings, vehicles, boats, and more.

You'll see us refer often to:

- **Downsizing To Go** → A full estate cleanout, usually in preparation for a sale, move, or transition.

- **Downsizing To Stay**→ Decluttering and improving safety for those staying in the home.

We cover both, but much of this book focuses on Downsizing To Go, since that tends to require the most effort. Don't worry—we'll always make it clear which advice applies to which scenario.

So, let's dive in!

Section 1
The Heart of Downsizing

Chapter 1
How Do You Approach Downsizing?

The "Family-Friendly Way"!

What is a "family-friendly" approach to downsizing? And does it matter?

A family-friendly approach views downsizing from the perspective of the family, not from downsizing experts or companies that do this as a business. It considers the emotions and feelings of family members—whether it involves making decisions about an estate after someone has passed, helping someone who can no longer make decisions, or simply downsizing to stay.

This approach ensures that the process supports the family, rather than being solely focused on making money, rushing through a fast cleanout, or ignoring certain family members because they are difficult to deal with.

This book is for those who want a practical guide to downsizing—one that balances efficiency with emotional consideration.

How Does It Work?

A family-friendly approach makes the process of decluttering and reducing possessions collaborative, respectful, and as stress-free as possible for everyone involved.

Okay, maybe not entirely stress-free, but at least a way to minimize the stress. Here are some guiding principles to help:

Tailored to Your Family

Every family is unique. That's why it's essential to adapt the downsizing process to fit your specific needs.

Don't worry—we'll guide you through creating a plan that works best for your family.

Involve the Right Family Members or Friends

Engage everyone in the process, ensuring that each person's voice is heard, especially regarding items with sentimental value.

This helps avoid conflict and makes everyone feel included in the decision-making process.

Some people will participate more than others, and some might not be able to—physically or emotionally. It may surprise you who struggles the most. Try to understand and avoid judgment.

Take a Planned, Practical Approach

Rather than rushing through, give space for emotional reflection—especially when handling heirlooms or personal possessions tied to memories.

Tip: There will be plenty to throw out on Day 1—we'll walk you through it later.

Create a clear plan and execute it thoughtfully.

Create Positive Memories

Turn downsizing into an opportunity to share stories and memories.

Even small gestures—like giving away meaningful items or sharing old photos—help keep family members engaged and make the process lighter.

Make It an Educational Opportunity for Kids

Involve children by teaching them about decluttering, managing possessions, and philanthropy.

Show them how donating items helps others and, of course, teach them that some things—like Hummel figurines—aren't as valuable as they once were.

Share Decision-Making

If one person wants to keep an item, while another thinks it should be sold or donated, come to a compromise together.

The goal is to avoid conflict and ensure everyone is comfortable with the outcome.

Take Your Time Sorting & Organizing

Some people cling to certain items from their past.

While you may want to move quickly, take time to locate the family items that were requested—even if it's just another stuffed animal or a used Queen concert ticket.

Be Tolerant—Keep the Family Together

Especially for Downsizing To Go (a full cleanout), be supportive of family members who struggle with the process.

People grieve differently, and some do so silently. Sometimes, it's more important to lead with compassion than logic.

And don't be surprised by the person who won't lift a finger to help —but still wants the patio set.

Finding the Right Approach to Downsizing

There are two extreme approaches to downsizing an estate:

- **Quick and Costly** Hire a company to handle everything—within days or weeks, the property is empty.

    Downside: Expensive, and most estate contents end up trashed, which can feel wasteful (but may be necessary in some cases).

- **Slow and Painful** You and your family go through every single item yourselves.

    Downside: It takes a long time, becomes exhausting, and is not always practical.

Most people don't want either extreme, which is why we focus on a balanced approach.

Sometimes, Extreme Solutions Are Necessary

Some situations require a fast, full cleanout, such as:

Hoarder Houses When the property is unsafe, infested, or falling apart.

Vacation Homes Second homes with few sentimental items (usually just old furniture).

Distant Relatives' Estates When there's no immediate family involvement.

Urgent Property Sales When a home needs to be emptied quickly for sale.

For most people, though, a balanced approach is best.

Evaluating a Property for Downsizing

When we first meet a client (usually during a sales call), we assess:

- The current state of the home and its contents.

- The number of family members involved.

- Any important deadlines or estate issues.

For example, we once handled an estate on the South Shore of Massachusetts.

- The owner had Alzheimer's, and his family recognized he couldn't manage the downsizing process alone.

- They hired us to help sort through the estate, despite the high cost.

- The house was filled with valuable collectibles, silver, gold, jewelry, and family heirlooms—so a detailed cleanout made sense.

- We even shredded 500+ pounds of documents from his old business records!

This was a multi-million-dollar estate, so taking the time to sort everything properly was worth it.

Most homes don't require this level of involvement, but the goal of getting value from downsizing can still be achieved without sorting through every single item.

What's Inside a House?

When downsizing, it's not just about space—it's about the sheer number of items in a home.

Clothing, books, paperwork, kitchenware—these are great starting points. Downsizing clothes first gives an instant sense of progress.

Once you see that progress, tackling the rest of the house becomes easier.

Final Thoughts

What do you really have to downsize?

That's what we'll dive into next.

Chapter 2
What's in a House?

The Valuable and Not So Valuable

What are we downsizing anyway? It's important to take a close look at a house or estate to understand what you're downsizing. In our business, it's become easy to step onto a property and determine the best approach because we have done it so many times.

But, if you haven't done downsizing before it can feel intimidating. Don't let it overwhelm you. Almost every house or property contains the same types of items, and many are easy to downsize.

Let's take a closer look. What's really in the house you're clearing? It's more than just a lot of stuff.

Understanding the Categories of Household Items

Typically, household items can be grouped into several major categories, which can help with organization, downsizing, or inventory management.

When estimating the percentage of items by sheer number, rather than by bulk or space, the distribution changes quite a bit. For an educated guess check out the table on the following page.

We'll bet you'll find that the items you're working with will be similar.

When you review the list, think about the items in the property you need to clean out. What will be your challenges? Collections of plates? Old magazines and newspapers? Books? Clothes? At first, you may think, "there's a lot of everything," but when you look closer, you will start to see the areas that will be the most work.

The Impact of Downsizing Top Volume Items

You may be surprised by how much decluttering can transform the home simply by eliminating or significantly reducing some of the top volume items. We'll dive into the details of the downsizing process a little later but think about how the home would look by just reducing some top volume items. Now that we've looked at the big picture of household contents, let's talk about what actually holds value.

Volume of items in the home

CATEGORY	VOLUME	ADDITIONAL INFORMATION
ART	Low	Determine value. Don't give away the Rembrandt!
ANTIQUES	Low-Medium	Being old doesn't make it automatically worth something.
CLOTHING & ACCESSORIES	High	Sell newer, consign special interest. Decide on designer items.
KITCHENWARE	High	Brand names & condition matter. Includes cooking & entertaining items.
ELECTRONICS	Low-Medium	Larger (TVs, computers, consoles) & smaller (clocks, calculators)
TOYS & GAMES	Low-Medium	Includes children's toys, board games, puzzles & recreational items.
DECOR	Medium-High	Anything that gives a home style: art, lamps, objects
BOOKS, MUSIC, & MEDIA	5-10%	Low value, sell or donate at volume unless vintage or unique
PERSONAL CARE	Medium-High	Toiletries, grooming, medications, makeup. Useally quite numerous
OFFICE SUPPLIES	5-10%	Home office items: including printers, paper, pens, desktop
HOBBIES & CRAFTS	0-10%	Can be anything from sewing to painting to wood carving
TOOLS & HARDWARE	1-5%	Hand tools are usually donated. Power tools sell well condition-dependent.
LINENS & TEXTILES	3-5%	Fabric items such as bedding, towels, curtains, rugs
FURNITURE	1-3%	Unless it's MCM or a special piece, most are difficult to sell
APPLIANCES	1-3%	Larger items usually stay with home. Smaller can be donated or sold
OUTDOOR & SPORT	1-3%	Includes sports equipment as well as patio items like grills, furniture & tools
CLEANING SUPPLIES	1-3%	Cleaning tools and products: Brooms, mops, detergents, etc.

What's Really Important and Valuable in Your Estate?

The most valuable items are the heirlooms and family items that have been in the family for years. But besides the heirlooms, what's really important and valuable in your estate? It varies from house to house, but there are some common themes. And yes, we will talk about what's not valuable too.

When evaluating a job, one of the first things we look at is the amount of furniture and big items, knowing they likely won't sell. Why? Large furniture is the hardest to get rid of and often sells poorly. At the time of this writing, and for the past few years, most furniture in Massachusetts hasn't been very valuable (e.g. traditional brown furniture, upholstered chairs and couches, china and display cabinets). If you're downsizing in a different area, check local demand for furniture before assuming it holds value. Pianos are another item that are difficult to sell and a pain to get rid of.

When downsizing an estate, it's crucial to identify items of potential value. While the specifics may vary by region or country, many of the valuable categories are the same. Let's dive in and explore what might hold value in the estate.

WHAT'S IN A HOUSE?

	What items have potential value	
CATEGORY	POTENTIAL VALUE	ADDITIONAL INFORMATION
ART	High	May need to consult with a service for valid appraisal
ANTIQUES	High	Condition and current taste dependent. May need dealer consult
CLOTHING & ACCESSORIES	High	Designer bags, clothes may hold value. Be aware consignment may keep you to time frame
JEWELRY	Medium-High	Best to find a trustworthy dealer for evaluations. Used fine jewelry is a tough sell
FAMILY HEIRLOOMS	Priceless	Keep and/or store. For you and upcoming generations
FURNITURE	Medium-High	Tastes vary per location. In general, brown & upholstered furniture are tough sells. Condition plays a large role.
COLLECTIBLES	Low-Medium	Well-known brands (Hummel, LLadro, Byer's have value, but not nearly as high as in the past.
BOOKS	High	Potential values include: first editions, signed by famous authors, rare, antique in good condition
MUSICAL INSTRUMENTS	Medium-High	Still in demand. Condition plays an important role. Pianos are near impossible
CHINA/ SILVERWARE	Low-High	Occasionally a set of china sells for a good price, but rarely. Silver can be sold as is or by weight
RUGS & CARPETS	Low-High	Handwoven and Persian rugs hold value. Consult local dealer

What's Not So Valuable

Here's a list of some items that rarely have a lot of value. Most times it's because they are easy to find and readily available, without an audience to buy them, i.e. a high supply vs. low demand drives value down.

Keep in mind that collectible markets can change often. Items that were once trendy or valuable might lose their worth when people lose interest or when there's too much supply. Unfortunately, much of the collectible market is over-saturated, which often leads to low prices or no value at all. This can vary by region, so it's a good idea to check your local market. However, in most cases, you'll likely see what we see every day: not much demand for certain collectibles from the past. And as with selling most things, condition is key. Even if a collectible is desired, its value depends on its condition.

WHAT'S IN A HOUSE?

What items usually have a lower value

CATEGORY	COMMENTS
MASS-PROD. FIGURINES	Hummel, Precious Moments and the like have diminished in value due to oversupply and change in taste.
STUFFED DOLLS & ANIMALS	Cabbage Patch Dolls, Beanie Babies and other stuffed collectibles have little-to-no value unless quite rare, in original packaging and in good condition
VINTAGE SPORTS & COMMON CARDS	The market has been over-saturated with this once-hot commodity. Cards older than the 80s & 90s may still hold value, otherwise let them go
COLLECTOR PLATES, SPOONS GLASSES ETC.	Current consumers have little taste for this category and rarely spend much on them
COMIC BOOKS	If it's not from the silver ages (pre-70s or older) or containing a major character debut, most modern comics do not appreciate as older ones did
FRANKLIN MINT	Although these items were sold as investments, they have not lived up to their promise
STAMPS	Unless it's a rare stamp, or one with an error, most stamps are worth less than their printed value
ANTIQUE SEWING MACHINES	Someone may love an antique Sears for its beauty, but older machines rarely retain value as they are relatively easy to come by.
LOCAL HISTORIC ITEMS	These items are great for preserving memories, but not for preserving value
COMMEMORATIVE COINS	We're talking mass-produced modern coins, such as those from the U.S. Mint etc. Overproduced, their value has dropped
MASS-PRODUCED TOYS 80s-90s	Star Wars & Transformers aside, most mass-produced items from the 80s & 90s aren't worth much, although original packaging and pristine condition help
ART	Most art consists of reproductions. Or not considered "fine" or high-level original art. Although art in the eye of the beholder, but don't expect much monetary return.
ANTIQUES	A piece that's in severe disrepair, is moldy or non-functioning, or is missing pieces will have considerabley less value
PIANOS	Sadly, pianos just don't sell. Better to donate to an organisation that needs one.
REGULAR BOOKS	Whether soft or hard cover, contemporary or popular books - as well as informational books of yore - are best to donate
COLLECTIBLE ITEMS	Tea cups, shot glasses, frogs, rabbits and other themed groups of items meant something to the original collector, but not so much to someone else
KITCHEN MISCELLANEA	Mismatched sets, random glasses and mugs, cut glass or crystal...all have little-to-no value.

What Can I Get Rid Of Right Away?

If you are itching to get going, here are some things that can be quickly and easily discarded:

Expired Items:

Pantry or Kitchen Items Expired food, old spices, and anything past its "best by" date.

Medications Expired or unused medicines (dispose of properly and safely please).

Cleaning Supplies Dried out or expired cleaning products.

Old Papers and Magazines:

Magazines and Newspapers Outdated magazines and newspapers that no one reads or references. There are not many magazines or even old newspapers that are worth holding on to. A Marilyn Monroe *Playboy* issue, or an Eddie Mathews *Sports Illustrated* are worth a few bucks. If you have a key issue or a collection you think may have value, do some research.

As with most items, condition is key. *National Geographic* magazines are a common save, but to be honest, they don't sell very well. Only specific issues have value.

Junk Mail

Broken or Unused Household Items:

Broken & saved pieces of items Cracked dishes, chipped glasses, or pots and pans with peeling coatings.

Small Electronics Old smaller electronic or battery-operated items that no one uses or that are obsolete, like cassette recorders, calculators, old music players, etc.

There are some niche items that have value, such as old voice recorders that ghost hunters use. So do some quick research if you need to. To be honest, we usually donate most of the small electronics after some quick research.

Duplicate or Excess Items:

Plastic Containers Excess food storage containers, especially those without matching lids.

Old Towels and Linens Worn-out or stained towels, sheets, and linens that are unlikely to be used again. Donate if they still are in good shape. If they are usable but not in great condition some animal shelters will take them.

Bathroom Products:

Old Toiletries Half-used or expired toiletries such as lotions, shampoos, and soaps.

Outdated Personal Care Items Expired or dried-out personal care items. It's usually a good size pile!

Clothing and Shoes:

Worn-Out Items Clothes that are stained, torn, or too worn to donate. Yes, it's time to get rid of the 80s T-shirts, unless it's a Grateful Dead or some other band that people collect. Some clothing can be sold.

Unusable Miscellaneous Items:

Old Batteries Expired or dead batteries (please recycle properly).

Outdated Accessories: Chargers, cables, or parts that no longer match any current devices (We keep them unidentified cables and chargers until the end of the job in case we find the unit the cable goes to).

Unused Manuals: Instruction manuals for items you no longer own. Since much of this information is online, there is no need to save the space-taking paper.

Empty Boxes from Purchased Items OK, we do like it when our clients keep boxes. That way we can pack an item back up if we sell it or donate it. But to be honest, getting rid of the empty boxes frees up a lot of space. If there's space in the home to keep empty boxes as you work, for later use, then keeping them as you go is a good option. If there is little space, best to clear them. Admittedly a tough choice.

Summary: What's Valuable and What's Not

In any downsizing project, one of the first challenges is figuring out what's truly valuable and what's not. This isn't just about financial value, it's also about sentimental value and practicality. Some items might have high market worth, like antiques, jewelry, or collectible art, while others might hold deep emotional significance even if they have little resale value. Conversely, many things that seem important in the moment might not be when we consider their actual usefulness or the cost of keeping them.

The key is to separate sentiment from practicality. As you sort through the contents of a home, furniture, keepsakes, clothing, tools, and more, you'll need to assess each item for its true value in your family's next chapter. This involves asking questions like: Will this be useful in the future? Does it fit into the space or lifestyle I'm planning for? Will it add meaningful value, either emotionally or functionally?

Once you've determined what's valuable and what isn't, it's time to take action. Downsizing isn't just about deciding what to keep; it's about implementing a plan to distribute the rest in a practical way. This could mean selling items of worth, donating things that could help others, recycling responsibly, or discarding what can't be used again. In this book, we'll guide you through each of these steps, providing you with the tools and strategies to complete your downsizing project.

From organizing estate sales to finding the right charities for donations, and making sure nothing falls through the cracks, we'll focus on actionable, step-by-step methods to turn decisions into results. Downsizing can be an emotional journey, but by taking a practical approach, you can transform a cluttered space into a peaceful, functional environment, one step at a time.

First things first, why are you downsizing and how do you start?

Chapter 3
Preparing for the Downsizing Journey

Why Downsizing?

Before we dive into the nuts and bolts (or should we say, boxes and bubble wrap?) of downsizing, let's talk about why you're doing this in the first place. Maybe the kids have grown up and moved out, leaving you with empty rooms and echoes of "Did you do your homework?" Or perhaps you're just tired of tripping over old toys, holiday decorations from twenty years ago, and that treadmill you swore you'd use (but has become a very expensive clothes hanger).

Or maybe you don't have a choice. Either way, it's time to get moving.

Downsizing will not merely clear your space. It will help clear your mind as well. It's a chance to let go of the clutter, both physical and emotional, and make room for new memories, and new adventures. Most of our clients are happy, if not relieved, when they have completed downsizing. Even with emotionally-complicated, tough jobs, the move in every case was the right thing to do. You want to downsize before you have to.

The Game Plan

Starting a downsizing effort often begins with a family or team meeting. It can be a meeting between the key people of the estate or the whole team if you have it assembled. Gather the team around (preferably at a table that's not already buried under stuff) and lay out the plan. If the family members are staying in the house, this is the time to emphasize why downsizing is happening: whether it's to make life simpler, prepare for a move, make safety improvements, or to reclaim valuable space. Frame it in a way that highlights the benefits, like less cleaning, more room for activities, stay in the home, or even the chance to make some extra cash from a yard sale or selling items.

Whether you start with a meeting depends on the situation. If you're Downsizing To Stay in the home, the focus will be on decluttering and reorganizing, with the owner having significant input on what stays and what goes. In this case, a family meeting can be a great opportunity to gather ideas and get everyone on the same page, since the changes will directly affect their day-to-day lives.

On the other hand, if you're Downsizing To Go, the approach often shifts to clearing everything out with fewer sentimental decisions. Sometimes, especially if emotions are running high, you may need to dive right in and adapt as you go. The key is to understand the type of downsizing you're tackling and adjust the level of collaboration accordingly. There is usually one person that takes overall charge of the downsizing project.

We know you're thinking, **"This sounds like a lot of work"**. You're not wrong. But here's the good news: you don't have to do it alone. Downsizing can be a team sport, and your family (and sometimes friends) can be your all-star lineup. Sorry for the sports analogy, but downsizing really is a team effort. Getting everyone on board might take some convincing (especially if you have a father who thinks their stuff is worth more than they paid for it years ago) but with a little teamwork, you'll all be high fiving over those empty shelves in no time. Or at least be giving a collective sigh of relief.

Envision & Establish Clear Goals

The key to successful downsizing is having a clear vision of what you want to achieve. Are you aiming for a minimalist look, or do you just want to be able to open your closet without an avalanche? Are you organizing a home that the family will continue to live in, or one that they will be selling? Whatever your goal, make sure it's clear, realistic, and shared with your team.

Remember, the ultimate goal is that this adventure is family-friendly, so be sure to involve everyone in setting priorities and goal posts. Even the youngest members of the family can have a say (just steer them away from goals like "turn the living room into a play area").

Once you've got your goals, write them down and put them somewhere visible like the fridge, next to the grocery list if you're downsizing your own lived-in home. Or where everyone gathers to get their organizing materials if you're downsizing a home that is not occupied. This will keep everyone motivated and on track.

And don't forget to celebrate the small wins along the way! Every bag of clothes donated, every shelf cleared, is a step closer to your goal. Plus, it's a great excuse for a pizza night.

Create Downsizing Stations

Set yourself up for downsizing success by first setting up one or two "Downsizing Stations" in your home: places where you can keep all your supplies organized and easily accessible. So, when you wonder "*Where's that packing tape?*" you'll actually know where it is! We pick a central place close to a door or a garage store the supplies. You could have several areas with downsizing supplies. Each station should include:

> **Cardboard Boxes** for donating, organizing, storage, gifting (get some free boxes, you'll need them.)

Packing & Scotch Tape for shipping items, shoring up old boxes, adding non-sticky labels, etc.

Trash Bags of all types (clear for items you'll want to see, black for trash, white for easy labeling)

Tools for Cutting, Measuring Scissors, matt knives, razor blades, tape measure

Paper Towels for cleaning things off or sopping up messes

Sharpies Medium is best. Bold for high visibility

Labels Sticky labels or tags. Also, white artist tape can work as a label.

Food Storage Bags Great for jewelry, small toys, scarves, etc.

Cleaning Items Window cleaner, sponges, brooms, mops and vacuum cleaners

Because a pile (or tower or deluge) of boxes can take up a lot of space, pick one or two large (and hopefully central) rooms, or a garage etc. where everyone can go to find the items that they will need on the days they are helping.

A word on boxes: be sure to have many cardboard boxes of different sizes at hand. You'll need big ones for things like winter coats and small ones for keepsakes. If you'll be storing items to keep in a basement or closet, have some plastic bins as well: clear ones for items you'd like to see easily (where's my red puffer jacket?). And be sure to have lots of Sharpies. You'll need to label everything! (Trust us, you don't want to accidentally donate your spouse's favorite sweater to the thrift store.).

Creating these stations is like setting up a base camp before climbing a mountain. (And just like any good base camp, it should have snacks). Downsizing is hard work, and you'll need to keep your energy up! And music, it's OK to lighten the mood. Once you get going, you will get in a rhythm.

A Note on Downsizing To Stay

If you're downsizing a home but still living in it, you'll have to decide what you need or want to keep. Obviously, it will be a pain to have to put things away every day, so it's best to have an out-of-the-way choice for your command center if you're still in the home! After a day's work of downsizing to stay we will put away and organize as much as possible to keep the home as neat and safe as we can.

Setting up Downsizing Toolkits

Before everyone jumps into action, they'll each need a Downsizing Toolkit. This isn't your typical hammer-and-nails kind of toolkit; it's very particular for downsizing. While the bulk of items will be in the Downsizing Station, each helper should have their own portable kit. This way, if someone is working on the bedroom and someone else in the garage at the other end of the house, they'll each have what they need.

Each kit (in a plastic bag or other container) should include:

- **Packing & Scotch Tape**
- **A Sharpie or two**
- **Small bunch of labels/tags**
- **Scissors**
- **Measuring Tape** Good for size reference if a far-away relative wants something, or if you plan to sell an item later, or if you need to know if an item can fit in a car

One more important item as you start your downsizing journey. For most jobs, we recommend you keep track of your valuable items in a simple inventory list.

How to Keep Track of Valuables (Emotional or Financial)

When dealing with a family group, it's best to keep an inventory of items that may be desired by several people, that may have monetary value or may be key in evaluating an estate, so they don't get "lost" in the shuffle.

Keeping everything organized during the downsizing process is crucial, but it's easy to get overwhelmed. Here's a simple inventory method to help keep track of the important stuff without creating more work than necessary. Remember: DO NOT INVENTORY EVERYTHING! You don't need to document every spoon or old magazine. Focus only on the key items, the ones with value, and err on the side of caution when deciding what's important.

Quick Inventory Method

Create a Simple Inventory Sheet: Use a notebook, spreadsheet, or app to list key items. Include columns for:

Item Description A brief description of the item.

Location Where the item is found in the house.

Sentimental Value Rate the sentimental importance on a scale (e.g., low, medium, high).

Financial Value Estimate the financial worth of the item (e.g., low, moderate, high).

Decision Choose from Keep, Donate, Sell, Recycle, or Trash.

Responsible Party

Tagging System: Use color-coded stickers to mark items:

Green: Keep. Most valuable items fit here
Yellow: Donate.
Blue: Sell.
Red: Trash/Recycle.

Focus on the Essentials Only inventory items that are valuable, sentimental, or need specific decisions made. Avoid getting bogged down with minor, everyday items.

Digital Option If you prefer, consider using an inventory app, but that's normally overkill for a single downsizing project. Excel, Google Sheets – or a large white board - work fine.

By using a combination of a simple inventory sheet, a visual tagging system, and key questions about each item's value, you can keep the downsizing process organized and efficient without getting overwhelmed. This way, you can focus on what really matters and move forward with confidence in your downsizing journey.

During the downsizing process, you'll find yourself asking, or being asked, the same questions over and over. This is especially true when working with seniors who may have memory challenges. One important thing to remember is to avoid saying things like, "You already told me that," or "Don't you remember?" These comments can come across as dismissive or frustrating.

Instead, simply answer the question patiently, even if it's the fifth time. A kind response doesn't take much effort, and it helps maintain a positive atmosphere.

Being family-friendly during downsizing means approaching the work with care and considering people's emotions and feelings. That's what makes downsizing so challenging: it's not just about the physical stuff, it's about navigating the emotions tied to it.

Let's take a quick look at why this can be so difficult. In the next chapter, we'll explore the emotional side of letting go and how to deal with those sentimental items that tug at your heart (or make you want to avoid downsizing altogether).

For now, take a deep breath, gather your supplies, and get ready to tackle the clutter, one room at a time!

Closet Confessions

The typical American woman's closet holds 103 items—yet many people still feel they have nothing to wear!

In fact, a significant portion of these clothes often go unworn for years.

Chapter 4
The Emotional Side of Downsizing

Why is this so hard?

Let's get real—downsizing isn't just about stuff. It's about letting go of memories, connections, and sometimes even a piece of identity. That's what makes it so hard. While it's easy to say goodbye to that old busted blender, it's a bit more of a challenge to let go of the photo albums, the kids' first drawings, or Grandma's favorite teapot. The whole downsizing thing can feel like breaking up with the past and getting rid of all the evidence!

But here's the thing: just because something's difficult doesn't mean it's not worth doing. In fact, the emotional challenges of downsizing are exactly what make it so rewarding. When these feelings are faced head-on, a new appreciation for what's truly important in your life is gained. And what can be let go of becomes so much clearer. So, grab a tissue if you need to, and let's talk about how to downsize without feeling like something's being lost.

Handling sentimental items

Okay, we know what you're thinking: *"How do we downsize sentimental items without, you know, crying into a pile of old yearbooks?"* Good question! The key is to approach sentimental items with a plan and a lot of kindness, for yourself and your family.

First, give permission to keep the things that really matter. If Grandmother's quilt gives a warm feeling, that's a keeper. But saving every greeting card ever received? That's not.

Here's the golden rule: Ask yourself, *"Does this item make me happy or serve a purpose in my life right now?"* If the answer is yes, it stays. If the answer is no, it might be time to let it go.

And remember, letting go doesn't mean forgetting. Take photos of items they want to remember but don't have space for. Or create a memory box for those smaller, meaningful objects. For collections, have them keep some of the most important ones, and "give" away the rest.

When you can, involve the whole family in this process. Share the stories behind the items and see if someone else in the family would like to hold on to that cherished heirloom. You might be surprised at how these conversations bring you closer together, even as you're letting go.

Overcoming resistance to change

Even when downsizing makes sense, resistance creeps in--whether from fear of change, attachment to 'the way things were,' or just not knowing where to start. It could be the fear of the unknown, or the attachment to the way things have always been. Whatever the reason, it's normal to feel a bit of resistance when downsizing.

The trick is to acknowledge these feelings without letting them take over. Remind yourself and your family of the benefits of downsizing which is more space, less clutter, and the opportunity to create new memories in a simplified home. Celebrate the small victories along the way and be patient with the process.

Downsizing: To Stay or To Go

Downsizing is an emotional thing, for sure. But by setting goals and communicating with everyone involved, a lot of the negatives can be avoided. Everyone knowing the "why" is key. Two simple breakdowns are whether you're Downsizing To Stay or To Go. Obviously, the two approaches will focus your efforts differently, each having its own emotional side. In both cases, communication is key. With your loved one who is entering a different phase of life, with yourself (if it's you!) and with anyone who's helping the process. Downsizing To Stay is often for safety and simplification reasons. For example, an elderly loved one needs to clear walking areas to prevent tripping. Or they don't entertain in the same manner as they did when they were younger, so 5 sets of dinnerware are definitely not on the table! Decades of holiday decorations are now sitting in layers of bins in the garage and attic. Your loved one's space needs to be lightened up so they are not possessed by their possessions.

The emotional side of Downsizing To Stay is that the person who's staying often likes their home just the way it is. So convincing them of how it can be better is the challenge.

One of the biggest priorities? Safety. Clearing walkways for walkers or canes, and making everyday essentials easier to reach. It helps to have a person who's trusted to sit down and explain how the changes will make things easier. An afternoon sorting out a kitchen cabinet so their favorite mug and snack plates are easily at hand will help start off the process.

Downsizing To Stay is best taken in bites. It's often good to start in an area where you can make a big visual change within a day or two. Tackling that kitchen is one of the most loathed jobs, but it can be extremely rewarding. Reducing from seven to one or two working frypans frees up a lot of space! And you can rearrange the essentials, so they are all easy to get to. And here's the chance to clear out any gadgets gathering dust, or duplicates. (Grandma isn't making anything in that George Foreman grill). Family members may take some unneeded items or can help sell groups of items on Facebook.

Although the change of minimizing "stuff" to make life easier is in itself a reward, it may be incentivizing to build in small celebrations *"We tackled the bathroom cabinet!"* with a trip to their favorite eatery. And don't forget to inject some humor into the situation. Downsizing doesn't have to be all serious and emotional. Make it fun! Play some music, have a downsizing party, or turn it into a game. Who can fill a donation box the fastest? Who can find the most ridiculous item that you forgot they even had? (Seriously, why do they still have that neon fanny pack from the '90s?)

We often find that family members resist the efforts of their spouses and children to reduce the number of items in the home. A friend or outside service can often break this logjam by sitting down and helping the person to focus on how they live now.

Downsizing To Go:

Let's give an example of things that come up when Downsizing To Go, meaning someone is moving from home. Say your Mom has to move to assisted living: an apartment. Currently she's in a large home. One family member lives nearby, and two are in different states. Each has a lot going on in their lives.

So logistics will come into play, as well as emotions. But this can be a wonderful way for the family to connect, even if it's over thousands of miles!

If everyone can come to the home to work for a few days, fantastic luck! As you all sort, encourage each family member to share their feelings about certain treasures, and listen with empathy. As you find yourselves stuck on some items, there may be compromises involved. You may have to find storage for Dad's beloved old rolling tool chest until everyone is ready to sell or someone is willing to take it. Mom may have to finally part with 8 of her 10 bins of Christmas carolers.

If relatives can't make the extended trip, family members that are in the house can shoot and share photos of any items that they may have emotional attachments to: clothes from the attic, an old yearbook or award. They can then arrange to send boxes of items to those people.

Managing different opinions

Not everyone will pitch in equally—some won't help at all. That's normal. Try not to keep a scorecard. Instead, focus on working with those who are willing. Please know this is a common occurrence. These kinds of life transitions can both help and hurt relationships. Please do remember to take care of yourself and take some time out as well.

Everyone holds their own opinions, and that is often magnified in transitional situations. Some families let one member be "in charge". Others switch on and off downsizing duty. Others split duties: one person gets the kitchen and the other the basement. In whatever ways you can, we encourage you to work together to achieve your ultimate goal.

Differences between family members who are more "minimalist" and those that are more "maximalist" will mean that it can be tough to decide what to keep and what to let go of. If the actual square footage of a new living space is smaller than the home, that makes decision-making easier. But when a downsizing person is choosing to stay, it's more a quality-of-life question. Again, a trusted friend or family member can often help in the process.

We have some wisdom from all our years downsizing countless homes. When downsizing, the goal is to find a balance between honoring the past and making space for the future. And if things get tense, take a break. Downsizing is a marathon, not a sprint, and it's okay to take it one step at a time.

What Do Our Clients Say After Downsizing?

We ask some of our clients, "What do I wish I had known before I started downsizing." Here are a few of their comments over the years.

"I wish I knew that all these collectibles I have been saving are not worth much anymore."

"I never realized how much stuff we had they we never used."

"I never thought my kids wouldn't want a thing of ours."

"I already feel better, what a relief. It was bothering me, not knowing what will happen to all my things."

"My family is happy we finally decluttered, but they didn't help."

"I wished I did it sooner, it wasn't bad at all. Having a process to downsize really helps."

"I could have never done it without you guys, sometimes it just makes sense to hire someone."

"I remember what this house looked like when we moved in."

"Wow, we can move around now."

"I can't believe my furniture didn't sell for much."

"I never knew it was so hard to give away things, I can't give this furniture away."

"I thought I would miss my collections, but it's actually a relief that they found a new home (footnote: she took the best ones with her)."

"Having all that stuff and not having a plan was giving me anxiety. I don't want to leave a mess for my family."

In almost every case, our downsizing clients experienced a huge sense of relief after the downsizing was complete. (Except for the client that couldn't believe their furniture and VHS didn't sell.) Many discovered things they didn't expect, whether it was the surprising lack of value in cherished collectibles, that their furniture was not sellable, or that their children did not want family heirlooms.

Some felt like a weight had been lifted, while others were struck by how much easier the process had become with a plan.

Through it all, these reflections remind us that downsizing is more than just a practical task; it's a transformative experience. We are always reminding people that downsizing is not about losing, it's about what they will gain: peace, clarity, and a renewed sense of purpose in a simplified home or a new home with less stuff. As for all those things? They were bought, used, and loved.

Now it's time to let go and move on. Remember, the emotional side of downsizing is just one part of the journey. It's okay to experience sadness or anxiety, just don't let those feelings stop you from moving forward. Soon, we'll get into the nitty-gritty of decluttering each room, and by then, you'll be ready to tackle it with confidence and even a smile. Keep going; you've got this!

Next up? Navigating family dynamics. We'll dive into the personalities you'll encounter--and how to keep things moving smoothly.

The Hardest Decision Is the First One

Most people avoid downsizing because they are afraid to make difficult decisions about sentimental objects.

Once they get started, they're usually surprised at how easy it becomes.

Chapter 5
Family Members We All Have and Love

And strategies to work with them!

We see a lot of family dynamics in the downsizing business, and it's always an adventure. Some family members jump right in. Others... disappear faster than you can say 'free stuff.' And that's okay! Downsizing is a stressful, emotional process that affects everyone differently. People react based on their own personalities, experiences, and relationships with the household and its belongings. Look at the emotional side of the effort and give them a break if they are having a tough time and can't jump right in.

Downsizing has a way of shuffling family roles. The one you thought would lead? Missing in action. The quiet one? Suddenly running the show. You'll be amazed at the shake-up. These dynamics can be frustrating, but they're completely normal. Every family has its quirks, and downsizing tends to bring those quirks to the surface. You might think a family member is avoiding work because they are lazy, but perhaps they can't handle it emotionally.

This chapter is about understanding the variety of personalities you'll encounter during a downsizing project. From the ones who seem to know everything (even if they don't) to those who get bogged down in sentimentality or even avoidance, there's a full spectrum of behaviors you'll need to navigate. Understanding these dynamics can help you approach the process with empathy and a sense of humor, rather than letting frustrations boil over.

Why does this matter? Because family dynamics can make or break a downsizing project. When emotions run high, conflicts can arise, and progress can stall. Recognizing these patterns can give you a better perspective and help you avoid taking things personally. Instead of letting personalities derail the process, you can use strategies to steer the project forward while keeping the peace. Keeping in mind you're just dealing with stuff and that the people are the most important helps guide your downsizing effort to avoid the pitfalls and problems we have seen over the years. Stuff is not worth fracturing a family relationship.

And yes, even as professionals in the downsizing business, we find ourselves in these roles from time to time. It's a reminder that no one is perfect, and everyone brings their own baggage, literal and figurative, to the table. Learn to manage family dynamics with patience and humor, ensuring the downsizing experience is as smooth as possible for everyone involved.

THE EXPERTS

THE ESTATE SALE KNOW-IT-ALL,
Professor Price Tag

This family member claims to know the exact value of everything from Aunt Mabel's teapot to the dusty stack of old *National Geographic* magazines. They think everything can be sold online at the price they paid for it.

STRATEGY: Use that enthusiasm. Ask them to focus on estimated pricing for items over a certain amount. (Those are usually the ones that cause family disputes.) Now if the "expert" has cleared one house or participated in clearing a house, that's great. If they did two, much better. If they want to do more after your property, have them call us.

THE SPREADSHEET STRATEGIST,
The Organization Overlord

They love color-coded lists, inventory spreadsheets, and timelines. To them, downsizing is a military operation. We love these guys as long as they stay engaged. Getting them to stay in the game is usually the problem.

STRATEGY: Take advantage of their skill set. Focus them on organizing lists of items considered valuable, or ones that are in dispute. Or ask them to develop a work schedule.

THE *"Maybe it's worth something"* APPRAISER,
The Treasure Hunter

Fearing missing a hidden fortune, they insist on getting every item appraised, including Aunt Edna's collection of ceramic frogs. (We do like frogs and they do sell, but not for much...unless they're gold frogs, which are surprisingly popular. Go figure!)

STRATEGY: Let them single out what they perceive as treasures: Hummels, LLadros, a Wedgwood teacup, or a Beanie Baby and encourage them to hunt away. But remind them that the proceeds will need to be shared.

THE GARAGE SALE DEVOTÉ,
The Yard Sale Optimist

They believe every item will sell for top dollar at a garage sale, even if it's a collection of mismatched Tupperware.

STRATEGY: Ask them to organize a yard sale and promote it via

Facebook, local signage and neighborhood word of mouth. Sometimes dealing with reality head-on is the best teaching device. Remind them: a yard sale is for mismatched mugs and old lamps—not Grandma's fine jewelry.

THE KEEPERS

THE SENTIMENTAL HOARDER,
The Memory Keeper
They can't part with anything because *"it reminds me of that one time…"* Even if it's just a broken spatula.

> **STRATEGY:** This person will not be about speed. Either assign them a small project like the kitchen drawer or have them go through Christmas items and never expect to see them again.

THE *"We can use this",*
Captain Upcycle
Always convinced that old furniture or random items can be repurposed, even when they're clearly broken or out of style. No, they won't refinish the old brown dresser (maybe someone will, but not anybody to help this project out).

> **STRATEGY:** Ask them to take the items they love that they are sure can be useful with repair. Or have them try to sell via Facebook or an online service. You may decide to let them have the proceeds if you were planning on disposing of it.

THE *"I'll take that, we bought it for them",*
The Claim Jumper
They come across items in the house that they bought for the family and want them back, as if it was a loan.

> **STRATEGY:** Hit 'em with the item, knock some sense into them. (Okay, not really) Be straight, tell them, *"You gave it to them. It's not yours."*

"That should be mine"!
The Entitled Thief
They think they should have been given the item, or they were once told (along with 20 others) that they will get the item, and they just take it. Sometimes the family knows the item's been lifted, sometimes not.

> **STRATEGY:** A general email to the group asking if anyone has seen the item in question. A private conversation and some nudging will sometimes help. Only get a lawyer involved if the item is of extreme value and the estate is in dispute.

THE OPPORTUNISTS

THE COLLECTOR,
The Freebie Fanatic
This person wants to claim every leftover item, regardless of whether they have space or any use for it.

> **STRATEGY:** Use the Project Charter (See Chapter 7). This is the agreed-upon way to distribute the items based on the wishes of the fam-

THE ONLINE AUCTIONEER,
The Digital Deal Maker
Always wanting to take items to sell online, convinced they'll strike gold with Grandpa's old VHS tapes or that box of vintage buttons.

> **STRATEGY:** Ask them to select their selected items right away and commit to a price. Remind them that the family will have to agree and that proceeds from their sale will have to be shared unless agreed upon otherwise.

DIVORCE LEFTOVERS,
The *"I left my high school letter jacket behind"* Joe
Sometimes the ex or their family shows up looking for things he or she left behind. It's pretty awkward and most times not appropriate. Although they shouldn't be there, they may show up from time to time.

> **STRATEGY:** Appoint a family member for them to communicate with. It may be necessary to organize specific days for them to go through anything that may be theirs. If it gets sticky, the lawyer for the estate may need to step in. Of course, if they are listed as part of the estate they will need to be in the loop and consulted on relevant decisions.

THE HELPFUL NEIGHBOR,
***"She promised me the lawnmower"* Larry**
This nosy neighbor is dying to get a hold of some free stuff. (We've experienced neighbors stealing items from an estate.). We like to joke around that it can be a frenzy, one neighbor tells another neighbor, and it becomes a free for all.

> **STRATEGY:** Make it clear that regardless of what they think, you are re-

quired to follow the law in distributing the estate property. Control access to the property since neighbors often have access to the property.

THE AGENT,
The *"I need one of those"* Nancy

Sometimes a nice family member tells the real estate agent to "take anything". And since agents have access, over time they may "shop" the estate. It can get quite messy if it's a free-for-all.

> **STRATEGY:** Make it clear that several family members must weigh in on any decisions and that you need to follow the law in distributing the estate property.

THE LET-IT-GOERS

TOM,
The Trash Tornado

Tom has one solution for everything: throw it out. If it's in his path, it's getting tossed. He moves fast and doesn't look back. But while his approach might seem efficient, it can also lead to regrets. Once it's gone, it's gone for good.

> **STRATEGY:** This is exactly why we don't start a downsizing job with a dumpster. Too many Toms out there, ready to clear out everything in one fell swoop. Remind Tom that downsizing isn't just about getting rid of stuff. It's about keeping what matters and letting go of the rest—thoughtfully.

THE SILENT SNEAKER,
The Ghost Declutterer
This family member doesn't have the patience for group consultations and often quietly removes items when no one's looking to avoid conversation, delays and potential conflict. The problem arises when they throw out the urn with Spot's ashes in it!

STRATEGY: During the "Sort & Organize" phase mark things clearly, so they are less likely to toss a wanted item.

THE EMOTIONALLY CHALLENGED

THE PERPETUAL POSTPONER,
Procrastinator Pete
This family member is famous for saying, *"We'll deal with it later"*, even as the downsizing deadline is looming.

STRATEGY: Accept that you will probably be the one to deal with "it". If their input is legally necessary, put it in a spreadsheet with decision dates and enforce deadlines.

THE EMOTIONAL BYSTANDER,
Tearful Tammy
These Tammys will shed a tear, sharing a story over every trinket, considerably slowing the process.

STRATEGY: Understand that they are not lazy or slow, they may just be having a hard time dealing with the stress of decision-making and letting go. Listen and empathize. And, if they slow down the process, give them a big box of old photos as their project to focus on and move yourself to another room.

THE DEPRESSED DE-CLUTTERER,
Dour Dan
For a number of reasons such as: hating house cleaning, objects reminding them of a lost family member, trouble making decisions, or a dust allergy... this person wants to be anywhere but helping downsize.

> **STRATEGY:** Understand that they may not be up to the task. Or give them a few boxes of things to go through at their home, like records or DVDs, if that's their thing.

THE WORK AVOIDER,
Lazy Larry
There are some people that are just plain lazy. If you have them on the team, don't rely on them for anything.

> **STRATEGY:** Coming out of the planning phase, make sure they understand that they won't have much of a role in the process. If they object, give them a concrete task (e.g. clear the basement closet) and see how they do.

Downsizing is a pressure cooker, and not everyone handles stress the same way. Expect surprises, try to roll with it, and—most of all—remember: stuff isn't worth breaking family ties over. You might be surprised at who has the toughest time, as well as who steps up.

The system will help you and yours get through it and hopefully have a little fun while you do. Remember to go easy on yourself, your family members and helpers. We encourage you to keep the family together no matter what role, good or bad, they play in the downsizing.

Section 2
Blueprint to a New Beginning

Chapter 6
The Downsizing Process in 4 Phases

How do you do it?

Downsizing an estate can feel like an overwhelming challenge, but with the right process it becomes a series of manageable steps. The next few chapters will guide you through each phase of the downsizing journey. We'll help you transform cluttered, chaotic spaces into a simplified, organized home that brings peace and clarity…or a cleaned out, empty house.

The method works both for Downsizing To Go (i.e. full cleanout) or Downsizing To Stay (partial downsizing).

After reviewing the categories of items in the home, you'll now use that information to help you go through the downsizing process.

This chapter is the outline of the process. The following chapters will spell each phase out in more detail.

The Downsizing Process: A Four-Phase Guide

The downsizing process is best approached in four phases: Plan, Sort & Organize, Distribute, and Fix & Final Cleanout. While these phases often overlap, following this process will make your downsizing effort much more manageable. You can use the process for the entire job or break it up into manageable sections and take it section by section. This is helpful for huge estates where a section might be a large barn or a full garage or basement.

Although you might feel tempted to jump in and start clearing things out right away, the best results come from starting with a little planning. In Chapter 2 we highlighted categories of items that can be discarded immediately for those eager to get started. Most people want to get started right away so if you focus on those categories of items we highlighted you're fine. While most downsizing projects don't require extensive planning, skipping this step can lead to costly mistakes. We've seen many situations where just a bit of planning could have saved significant time and money. So, the first phase is to do some planning.

PHASE 1: Plan

By this time, you have cleared out half the house, just kidding. The first phase of downsizing is to get the right team together and create a plan for your downsizing project. Keep in mind that not everyone in the family needs to be involved right away, or even at all. In this process, there are participants (the ones actively doing the work) and stakeholders (those who stay informed but aren't directly involved). Yes, the stakeholders are the lucky ones! But let's face it, someone has to roll up their sleeves and get the job done. Here are the key steps to planning. We will review in more detail in the planning chapter.

THE DOWNSIZING PROCESS IN 4 PHASES

Key steps to begin:

Define the goal Are you selling the property, making room for a family member, or simply downsizing to stay? Clarity here will save time later.

Assemble the team Focus on people who can and will help.

Draft a schedule Even a rough plan will make a big difference in keeping everything organized.

Create an email list Update the parties periodically with progress. Formally or informal, communication is the key. As with most things.

Create a simple Project Plan and Charter It's a great way to start the effort and make sure everyone is on the same page.

While setting the family team up for a successful downsize, we highly recommend producing two key documents: the Project Plan (The "Roadmap") and the Project Charter (The "Agreement"). The Project Plan is a detailed schedule with assignments, while the Project Charter acts as a contract outlining downsizing goals.

Here are a couple samples, but we'll go into more detail in the following chapter.

PHASE 2: Sort & Organize

The second phase is a fun one. Here is where you go through the property and determine what to do with everything. (Yes, you can continue to throw stuff out, too.) Begin by evaluating the entire home, identifying essential, sentimental, and non-essential items. We like to look at a property as spaces which correspond to rooms /areas of the house (e.g. living room, attic). Create sorting zones by clearing areas for boxes and bags where you will label items to keep, donate, sell, or discard. Group items by categories such as electronics, furniture, clothing, and kitchenware. This phase makes decisions easier, helping you determine what stays and what goes.

Evaluate Take a look at the house and get a sense of the essential, sentimental, and non-essential items.

Designate Select specific areas for items to keep, donate, sell, or discard. This helps in visualizing the downsizing process. There will be many sorting zones. A sorting zone could be a box for miscellaneous items per room. It could be an area of the room. Many times, we will have several labeled donation areas throughout the house, we can always pull something out of the donate pile if we need to. We can make a final determination during the distribute phase when we do donation runs.

Group by Category Organize items by categories like electronics, clothing, kitchenware, etc. This makes decisions more manageable and systematic. For example, if the house doesn't have vintage or designer clothing (like my stuff), just get it all together and pick a donation organization to give it to. We ask the clients who they prefer.

PHASE 3: Distribute

Once everything is sorted, whether it's an area of the house or the entire house, it's time to give each item its next home. Donate useful items to charities or local organizations that can put them to good use. Sell valuable pieces through an estate sale, yard sale, or by listing them individually. Finally, pass along sentimental or heirloom items to family and friends who will treasure them. This phase is all about finding the right destination for everything, ensuring nothing goes to waste and each item brings value to its new owner.

Donate Identify charitable organizations or individuals who could benefit from donations. Prioritize local or community-based options.

Sell Depending on the items, have an estate sale, sell individual items, or have a yard sale. We'll talk about the details in a later chapter.

Gift Offer sentimental or heirloom items to family members or friends who value them

PHASE 4: Fix & Final Cleanout

After distributing the items, arrange for the removal of any remaining items by hiring a dumpster or junk removal service. Make sure this lines up with any move-out date, or sale deadlines. Usually at the end there is some furniture that didn't sell, and no one wants, a ton of little stuff. Perform a final walkthrough to ensure nothing is left behind, and then clean the property thoroughly, or hire a cleaning service to prepare it for the next occupants. Here are the final steps:

> **Complete renovations** or repairs such as safety improvements.
>
> **Arrange removal of final items** Hire or schedule a service for bulk item removal (e.g., dumpsters, junk removal services). Ensure this is aligned with any property closing or move-out deadlines.
>
> **Final Walkthrough** Do a full sweep—check closets, drawers, and behind furniture. Make sure nothing important is left behind before calling it done.
>
> **Clean** Perform a deep clean of the estate or hire a cleaning service to ensure it's ready for the next occupants, or to meet sale or rental agreements.

The next couple of chapters look at the downsizing process in more detail.

Let's start with the planning phase!

Chapter 7
Phase 1: Plan

Start Things Out Right

A little planning upfront makes the whole downsizing process easier. Trust me, it's worth it. When it comes to downsizing, the planning phase is where everything starts to take shape. You wouldn't set out on a road trip without some type of map, and downsizing a house is no different. Taking some time to create a solid plan will save you a lot of headaches down the road and keep everyone on the same page. Plus, it helps set clear expectations, so you'll know what's coming up next and who's responsible–and not responsible–for what. Clear communication is important in keeping the family at bay, and happy.

As we touched on in the previous chapter your planning effort has two important work products: the Project Plan and the Project Charter.

The Project Plan and Project Charter can be simple documents hand, drawn or electronic, depending on the complexity of the downsizing effort. First, start with the Project Plan.

The Project Plan "The Roadmap"

Your Project Plan is the GPS for downsizing—it tells you what happens, when, and who's responsible. Without it, you'll be driving in circles. It's like planning a big trip, you figure out the route, the stops along the way, and the timing, so everything goes smoothly. It can be a simple list or a more detailed project plan using a chart.

Create Your Project Plan

First things first: you need to put together a basic plan. This is will be your reference during the entire downsizing process, so you want to make sure it covers the key steps. Start by asking yourself what the goal of this downsizing effort is. Are you clearing out a home to sell it? Making space for a new family member to move in? Or perhaps it's about getting rid of clutter and creating a more manageable living space. Whatever the reason, defining your goal is step one.

Once you have your goal in mind, break the project into the four downsizing phases: Plan, Sort & Organize, Distribute, and Final Fix & Cleanout. Think about how much time each phase might take and consider any deadlines, like the closing date of a home sale or a family move-in date. This plan doesn't have to be super detailed yet; you just need a rough outline to guide you.

It's best to have a physical plan that your team can refer back to as the downsizing effort progresses. Ideally, it's something you all sign off on, but is flexible enough that it can change as circumstances change (and they will!)

It can take the form of a digital detailed Gantt chart or a hand-written agreement.

If you are not familiar with a Gantt chart, they have a simple structure:

DOWNSIZING PROJECT	ASSIGNED TO	WEEK 1	WEEK 2	WEEK 3	WEEK 4	WEEK 5	WEEK 6	WEEK 7	WEEK 8
PHASE ONE: PLAN									
Create Project Plan									
Determine Family/Friends Team									
Create Project Charter									
PHASE TWO: SORT & ORGANIZE									
Room by Room Assessment									
ID Keep, Donate, Sell, Trash, Recycle, Dispose									
Identify Heirlooms, High Value Items									
Document What to Keep/Family									
PHASE THREE: DISTRIBUTE									
Donate Items									
Recycle Items									
Separate DIY Sale Items									
Separate Estate Sale Items									
Distribute Family Items									
PHASE FOUR: FIX & FINAL CLEANOUT									
Dispose of/Trash Items									
Take Recycle Items Away									
Make Donation Runs									
Clear Property of Items									
Broom Sweep Home									

Timeline on the top, projects phases on the left. For example, the Plan phase will take a day or two; Sort & Organize a little longer depending on the estate; Distribute takes the longest; and the last phase is Fix & Final Cleanout.

Although having an electronic file allows you to keep remote stakeholders in the loop, it may work better for your team to have an on-site white or chalk board. If so, your Project Plan could look like this:

Along with the Project Plan create a Project Charter.

The Project Charter or "The Agreement"

The Project Charter is your downsizing contract—a simple agreement that spells out the overall plan. It's where you decide on the goal, the rules, and who's in charge of making decisions.

Everyone signs off the agreement so you're all on the same page before the real work begins. It helps everyone involved know exactly what's going on and what's expected of them. It can be a simple document, a sheet of notes, or a detailed spread sheet.

For instance, if you're downsizing for Mom and Dad, the charter might say:

The goal is to move them to a smaller, more manageable home.

Jane will coordinate the sorting process.

We'll agree to communicate weekly and not throw anything away without permission.

The charter is a summary of the effort so everyone knows the goals and their role. It includes:

Objective Downsize the household for sale or relocation, ensuring a well-organized process.

Scope & Timeline Includes sorting belongings, coordinating distributions, and providing final cleanout services. When the downsizing needs to finish. Whether age-in-place improvements will be required.

Key Challenges For instance, volume of items, limited availability of donation centers, remote relatives.

Team Members Family members, downsizing specialists, and other involved parties.

Possible Vendors Vendors that may be part of the downsizing effort

This charter should be clear enough that everyone understands the plan and their part in it. What are your goals? A goal may seem simple, such as clearing Uncle Bob's and Aunt May's house, but it is usually more complicated. Finding old heirlooms, keeping the family peace, or preparing the house for senior living (i.e. age in place) might be some of your goals. Make sure the family is on board, or mostly on board, with the goals and the process. Finally, having the project charter, in whatever form, gives you a great start in your downsizing efforts by establishing your goal, the team that will accomplish it, and the vendors that can help.

Here's a template for the charter:

PROJECT NAME:
Start Date:
Prepared by:

PROJECT OBJECTIVE
The purpose of this project is to effectively downsize the household of [Your family], preparing it for sale, donating or relocation. The primary objective is to sort, organize, distribute and clean out all personal belongings, ensuring a smooth transition for the client.

PROJECT SCOPE
PHASE ONE: Plan
PHASE TWO: Sort & Organize
PHASE THREE: Distribute
PHASE FOUR: Final Fix & Cleanout

    OUT-OF-SCOPE
    • List out-of-scope items (such as shipping of large furniture, etc.)

KEY OBJECTIVES
• Fully downsized & organized home, ready for sale or turnover
• All personal items sorted, organized, distributed per client wishes
• Disposal and donation of unwanted items
• Broom clean home post downsize

BUDGET & DEADLINES
Ex: Downsize by x date
Ex: Estate account pays for the work

RISKS & CONCERNS
• Delays due to client decision delays
• Additional time due to high volume of items/specialty items
• Proximity and availability of donation centers may impact timing

KEY PEOPLE AND BUSINESSES
• Contact Info for key family members, businesses (like estate sale companies, disposal and donation services)

PROJECT APPROVAL
This project is approved by these individuals, and any changes will require additional approval

Get Approval from the Right People

Once your Project Charter is written, the next step is to get it approved by the appropriate parties. This could be family members, estate executors, real estate agents, or anyone else with a stake in the downsizing process. Getting their buy-in upfront is important because it helps avoid confusion and disagreements later. You want to make sure everyone's on board with the plan before any work starts.

Share the Project Charter with the people who will be involved and give them a chance to review it. Encourage them to ask questions or suggest changes and be open to their feedback. Once everyone agrees on the plan, you'll have a clear path forward, and the entire downsizing process will run much more smoothly.

Special Consideration if Aging-in-Place (Downsizing To Stay)

It's Time to Figure It Out

If a senior family member is staying put, now's the time to make safety upgrades--before an accident makes the decision for you. These upgrades can help make your home safer, more accessible, and comfortable as they age. While some improvements may be expensive, they're often more affordable than the long-term costs of assisted living.

Here's a look at what aging in place might involve and some of the key components to consider. Every situation is unique, so the costs will vary depending on the type of improvement and whether you'll hire a professional or will do it yourself.

Sometimes, staying in your home is the best solution and with the right modifications, it can be a safe and practical one. Take a look at the following table for some examples and the difficulty level to implement each. We encourage you to get a professional to do the estimates for your project.

As you can see, aging in place can be expensive if you do everything, but many improvements you can be made at a reasonable price. Getting a professional to help you evaluate is key. See the Fix & Final Cleanout chapter for more information on aging in place.

Safegaurding the Home			
ROOM	IMPROVEMENT	PROJECTED COST	DIFFICULTY
BATHROOM	Install grab bars near toilet and shower	$	Low
BATHROOM	Add non-slip mats in shower	$	Low
BATHROOM	Replace tub with walk-in shower	$$$$$	High
LIVING ROOM	Remove throw rugs or secure them	$	Low
LIVING ROOM	Add motion sensor nightlights	$	Low
KITCHEN	Lower countertop heights	$$$	Medium
KITCHEN	Move frequently-used items within easy reach	$	Low
KITCHEN	Install automatic shut-off for stove	$$$	Medium
BEDROOM	Install bed rail for support	$	Low
BEDROOM	Raise bed to ease getting in and out	$	Low
HALLWAY/ STAIRWAY	Add handrails on both sides of stairs	$$$	Medium
HALLWAY/ STAIRWAY	Install non-slip stair treads	$	Low
ENTRYWAY	Install a ramp for wheelchair access	$$$$$	High
ENTRYWAY	Widen doorways for wheelchair access	$$$$$	High
GENERAL/ HOMEWIDE	Improve lighting throughout the house	$	Low
GENERAL/ HOMEWIDE	Install smoke and CO2 detectors with alarms	$	Low

Keeping everyone in the loop

Communication makes or breaks the process. At minimum, send updates at the end of each phase so no one's left in the dark. So, to complete the planning phase, you might send out a note similar to the following.

Email 1: End of Planning Phase

Subject: We're all set to begin!

Hello [Family Member/Team],

> Good news! We've wrapped up the planning phase and are ready to roll! We've got a solid roadmap laid out, a team in place, and everyone on the same page. The next step is diving into the Sort & Organize phase, it's time to roll up our sleeves!
>
> We have selected a company to help us out, Caring Transitions of South Shore Massachusetts, along with a consignment shop down the Cape and a jeweler for the silver set and jewelry.
>
> The family team includes me managing the project, Uncle Bill and Aunt May, and their kids.
>
> Thanks to everyone for their input and patience so far. Let's get ready to tackle the clutter, uncover some treasures, and make this as smooth as possible.
>
> If you have any questions or concerns, please don't hesitate to reach out. Onward to the next phase!
>
> Warm regards,
>
> [Your Name]

Ready for the Next Phase: Sort & Organize

With your Project Plan and Project Charter in hand, you're ready to roll. The Plan phase might not feel as exciting as diving into the Sort & Organize phase, but it's the foundation for everything that follows. A well-thought-out plan will keep things on track and ensure that everyone is working toward the same goal. Plus, having the Project Charter in place means you won't have to worry about any last-minute surprises or misunderstandings.

Downsizing a home can feel like an enormous task, but with a simple plan in place it becomes much easier. The first step is to get your team together—there will be the people who actually do the work and, of course, the stakeholders who get to watch! You'll want to set a primary goal, whether it's selling the house or clearing it out for someone new to move in. Once that's decided, create a rough schedule to keep things on track. It doesn't have to be perfect, but having a plan gives you a good roadmap to follow.

Next, Phase 2. How do you sort & organize an estate? Do you have any colored dots?

Time to get your supplies and dig in.

The Clutter Paradox

Studies have shown that decluttering can reduce housework by 40%.

Less stuff means less time spent cleaning, organizing, and maintaining the home, making the whole house feel more manageable.

Of course, if you don't do housework you can safely ignore this paradox.

Chapter 8
Phase 2: Sort & Organize

The Key to Downsizing Happiness

You are off to a great start with a Project Charter and Plan. Whether your plan is napkin-based, or more formal (which we'd recommend), it's on to the nuts and bolts of finding value and clearing the property in a family-friendly way. Seems like "family-friendly" would be an obvious goal, but you would be surprised. We have seen fine art given to strangers, houses open for a free-for-all, and many other situations that have been not good for the family.

Downsizing is all about creating clarity, both in the home and for the family. The Sort & Organize phase is where the magic happens. It's not just about moving things from one place to another; it's about making intentional decisions about what stays, what goes, and what finds a new home. This is where you uncover hidden treasures, honor family history, and lay the foundation for a smooth and successful downsizing journey.

Sorting and organizing doesn't mean you have to go through every single piece of paper, examine each knick-knack, or analyze every small item in detail. Instead, it's about making intentional decisions on a broader scale. Focus on larger, more obvious items first, then the things you can sort quickly into keep, donate, sell, or discard. This approach helps you build momentum and develop a rhythm, making the process feel smoother and less overwhelming.

As you progress, you'll find that decisions come more easily and naturally. For example, when faced with a pile of old magazines or a drawer full of random papers, you don't need to painstakingly review every page. Instead, set aside items like these for later or designate them as recycle or trash. The key is to keep moving and not get stuck on the small stuff. Sorting is about progress, not perfection, and maintaining a steady pace is what will carry you through.

Think of the sorting phase as triage for a home: breaking a massive task into manageable chunks one room (or even one corner of a room) at a time. The goal is to create momentum and tackle the process in a way that feels achievable and, dare we say, even enjoyable.

So, grab your Project Plan, assemble your supplies, and rally your team. It's time to dive in. With a clear goal and the right mindset, sorting and organizing can become one of the most rewarding parts of your downsizing project. Let's get started!

Start with your Plan, Team, and Supplies

Grab a notebook or your phone and jot down the areas you want to tackle first. Think about which areas will be easier to handle, and which might need more time or help. The goal is to start with easier spaces to build some momentum. You'll feel accomplished as you check off each area! As a reminder from Chapter 3, here are some of the supplies you will be needed in your downsizing work:

Boxes & Containers for donating, organizing, storage, gifting

Packing & Scotch Tape for shipping items, shoring up old boxes, adding non-sticky labels, etc.

Trash Bags of all types (Clear for items you'll want to see, black for trash, white for easy labeling)

Cutting Tools Scissors, matt knives, razor blades

Paper Towels for cleaning things off or sopping up messes

Sharpies Medium is best. Bold for high visibility.

Labels & Dots Sticky and/or tags work. Also, white artist tape can work as a label.

Food Storage Bags Great for jewelry, small toys, scarves, etc.

Cleaning Items Window cleaner, sponges, brooms, mops and vacuum cleaners. Use what's in the house if available since you can't do much with used cleaning supplies.

The Dot System: Green/Red//Blue/Yellow

While we hate to give away our most secret of secrets, we will. Out of all the technology available to us, the best tools (besides trash and recycle bags) are dots. Those little packs of green, red, blue, and yellow sticky dots. Here's the system we use with our clients:

Green Keep for family
Red Dispose (trash/recycle)
Blue Sell
Yellow Donate

Remember when using dots don't stick them on something that could get damaged (e.g. a painting. Put them on the frame or back).

That's it, simple and very effective. We recommend a similar system. You don't have to put a dot on every item, just the big or important ones. Now that you have your dots (or some means to tag items) and your supplies. Let's get at it.

Divide and Conquer: Room by Room, Area by Area

The best way to tackle sorting and organizing is to divide the house into manageable sections. Looking at the entire house as one giant project can feel overwhelming. Instead, break it down into smaller areas. An area could be a room, attic, shed, garage, barn, or even a specific section of a larger space.

Start with spaces that hold less sentimental value. For example, the living room, dining room, or guest bedrooms are often easier to sort than the master bedroom or family room, which may be packed with personal items and memories. Leaving these tougher spaces for later helps you build momentum and confidence as you progress. As a business, we like to start with the master bedroom because we know it must be done and is usually the toughest of the bedrooms. It's your choice. But to be honest, every room will have to be tackled, so start with what's comfortable.

When you walk into a room, begin with a quick scan. Look for the big, obvious items that immediately stand out. You might notice things like an old chair that hasn't been used in years, piles of magazines, or decorative knick-knacks gathering dust. These are perfect candidates for your "donate" or "trash" piles. Place these items into your designated areas or boxes for keep, donate, sell, recycle, or trash. Remember to use your tagging system to label items.

Work Your Way In: From Large to Small

Once you've dealt with the larger, obvious items in the room, move on to the smaller details. This means opening drawers, cabinets, and closets. In these spaces, you'll often find dusty forgotten or unused items, perfect candidates for the "dispose" or "donate" categories.

Take your time with these smaller items but don't get bogged down. If you come across something sentimental or that you're unsure about, put it in a "miscellaneous" box. This box is for items you'll revisit later once you've completed the initial sort. The goal at this stage is to maintain momentum while making quick, confident decisions whenever possible. It may seem counter-intuitive to sort items in "miscellaneous" twice: first when you put items in the box, and then second when you re-visit them. But if you think there may be a treasure or two along with what it often junk drawer items, the miscellaneous box will be your friend, helping to keep momentum without missing an important item.

Keep Moving and Stay Efficient

Efficiency is key in the Sort & Organize phase. While it's important to be thorough, avoid getting stuck in one area for too long. Keep moving and maintain a steady pace. Take frequent breaks, this work can be emotionally and physically draining. Take your time to treat yourself right.

By the end of this step, you'll start to see the house taking shape. Rooms will feel (and look) lighter, and you'll have a clearer picture of what's staying and what's going. Sorting and organizing is not just about clearing clutter; it's about creating a new beginning, one decision at a time.

Identify Areas Requiring Specific Help or Knowledge

Some areas you will need to assign to specific family or team members. That person may have more interest, expertise or history with that specific category such as: jewelry, safes, financials, or filing cabinets full of necessary documents. Make sure you give that person enough time, especially if they are older and need assistance.

Save the Tough Spots for Later (or for Helpers!)

There are certain areas of the house that aren't as physically easy to maneuver such as basements, attics, garages, and sheds. These spaces can be full of old tools, forgotten items, and things that haven't been touched in years. They can also be dirty and cluttered, making them overwhelming to sort through. The good news? You don't have to tackle these tough spots right away, or even on your own. Consider leaving these areas for family members or friends who don't mind getting their hands dirty. If you know someone who enjoys organizing or loves a challenge, ask them to pitch in for these tougher spaces. They can help sort through old boxes, unused furniture, or even rusted garden tools. Just remember to provide your helpers with the same sorting setup, bags for recycling, trash, and boxes for donations or things to keep.

How to Start Each Room

As you go from room to room, make sure you're prepared before you dive in. Start by clearing a space near the door where you can set up your supplies. Place your recycling bags, trash bags, and boxes within easy reach. When you begin, take it one item at a time, and don't feel like you have to rush. Sorting through a lifetime of belongings can take time, and that's okay. Start with the larger items, then work your way through drawers and smaller spaces. If you're not sure about something, place it in the miscellaneous box and come back to it later. The goal is to keep things moving without getting stuck on any one decision.

Tackling Closets

Closets can be overwhelming, but they're often filled with a mix of essential and forgotten items which do not have a lot of value anymore and are easy to donate or dispose of. Here's how to approach closet spaces:

Start Small Begin with the hanging clothes. Use the "one-touch" method and decide whether each item will be kept, donated, or discarded.

Seasonal and Sentimental Items Often, closets contain off-season clothing or special-occasion outfits. Create a box for sentimental items you're unsure about for now. For seasonal clothing, consider donating if it hasn't been used in years.

Shoes and Accessories They are often overlooked, but they take up space. Limit shoes to pairs that are frequently worn and donate or discard the rest. Keep donation boxes and trash bags nearby so you can sort items as you go. Closet space is prime real estate, so be selective about what gets to stay when you are Downsizing To Stay.

Sorting Through Dressers and Drawers

Bedroom Go top to bottom on sets of drawers. Top drawers typically hold frequently used items, sort through these first. Keep only essential items like eyeglasses, medications, or daily-use electronics.

Sentimental Jewelry or Keepsakes For jewelry or keepsakes, set aside a "sentimental" box. Later, these can be distributed to family members or stored safely.

Clothing Drawers Similar to closets, go through clothing drawer by drawer. Items that haven't been worn in years or no longer fit should be donated. Fold or neatly store what remains.

For Downsizing To Go, we ask our clients where they would like us to donate clothing. Clothing is easy to donate. Just make sure it's in usable condition. You can also sell some clothing, shoes, and accessories in an estate sale.

Kitchen Drawers and Cabinets Set aside an open area and pull everything out of the drawer/cabinet. Group like items so you can determine duplicates and when to keep/donate/toss. Groups of items can be put together for an Estate or Garage Sale

Keep It Manageable

Remember, this process doesn't need to happen in one day or even one weekend. Downsizing is a journey, and the more organized you are with your sorting and organizing, the smoother it will go. By tackling the house room by room, you'll make steady progress and feel good about the work you're doing.

However, as we said above, it's okay to save tougher areas like attics, garages, basements, or sheds for later. These spaces tend to be overwhelming because they often hold a mix of sentimental items, forgotten treasures, and clutter. But don't feel limited, if you're ready to tackle one of these spaces earlier, go for it!

Garages: Our Favorite Storage Location

Using the garage as a temporary storage area can work brilliantly. The challenge, however, is clearing out the garage itself—a task that can be overwhelming and, let's be honest, sometimes unpleasant. Here's how to tackle it effectively:

> **Start With a Quick Scan** You've stared at that crowded garage a thousand times, but now it's time to clear it. First, identify large, obvious items that can be dealt with immediately, like old furniture, broken tools, or empty boxes. These can often go straight to the trash or recycling. Typically, there are many unused and outdated items that can be thrown away immediately.
>
> **Divide and Conquer** Break the garage into zones. Yes, even if it's a small garage you can still think of it in zones. For example, focus on one corner or section at a time. This prevents the feeling of being overwhelmed by the sheer volume of items.
>
> **Organize Into Categories** As you work, sort items into clear categories: Keep, Donate, Trash, Recycle. Use sturdy bins or boxes to keep

everything organized. The categories for garages tend to be: car-related items, home upkeep, lawn care, tools, paint, cleaning products, and outdoor holiday décor.

Dispose of Hazardous Materials Many garages contain items like old paint, chemicals, or batteries. These require special handling and should be taken to a local hazardous waste disposal facility (not as easy as it sounds). Latex paint can be tossed if dried out.

Check for Valuables Garages often hold forgotten treasures, like tools, sports equipment, or collectibles. Set these aside for family review or potential sale.

Clean as You Go Once a section is cleared, sweep or vacuum the area to keep things tidy. We like to clean each area after it's clear. Not a deep clean, but it will look and feel better once an area is cleared. This also makes it easier to use the garage as a staging area for the downsizing process.

Set Up Temporary Zones Once the garage is cleared, designate specific areas for items destined for donation, recycling, trash, or family review. Label these zones clearly to keep everyone on the same page.

By clearing and organizing the garage early in the downsizing process, you create a functional space that simplifies the rest of the project. It can become your central hub for sorting and staging items, making the entire downsizing journey smoother and more efficient.

The key is to keep moving forward at a pace that works for you. Every item sorted is a step closer to a lighter, more organized home, and that's a great feeling.

"I Need to Sort Everything"

Some people feel the need to go through every single item during the downsizing process. We've found that the best "cure" for this is to focus them on a few boxes or items, usually paperwork, photos, or sentimental family belongings, and let them go through them at their own pace. After a few hours, something remarkable often happens. They realize they don't need to go through everything! For some, this realization comes within an hour; for others, it may take longer. But eventually, they come to understand that they don't have to sort every item themselves, and that others can help make thoughtful, good decisions for them.

One of the keys to sorting and organizing is identifying the valuable items in the estate. These items may be valuable for sentimental reasons or monetary worth. Let's spend a little time talking about the ever-important heirlooms.

Heirlooms are simply special items that are passed down from one generation to the next, often because they have sentimental value, monetary worth, or represent family history. How do you handle them?

Special Considerations for Family Heirlooms, Sentimental, & High-Value Items

Family heirlooms are tricky. They're more than just objects; they're pieces of your family's history. But choosing to downsize means it may be time to make some tough choices. Heirlooms are in a category by themselves for potentially three reasons: They have emotional, monetary or historical value. Let's discuss the ways to consider your heirlooms.

Emotional Value

Here's where a family can really get bogged down. Let's assume you're downsizing a home that you will be selling, and all items must be removed from the home at the end of the process.

That means photos, documents, awards, costumes, furniture, decorative items, jewelry, clothing…you see where we're going here?

Put yourself in that position. When you pick up that photo, when you take Grandma's homemade quilt out of the drawer, how do you decide what to do with it?

Get Everybody Involved

Make sure everyone that should have a voice, does have a voice. This way, everyone gets a say, and no one ends up feeling left out. This part of the process is all about everyone feeling they have a fair piece of the pie. And if no one wants Aunt Edna's giant porcelain cat collection, it's okay to let it go.

A Downsizer's Dilemma - Photos, Home Videos, and Slides

It's an arduous process going through paper photos, videos, and slides, but if one of you is good at it, all the better. That person can sort photos depending on who is in them and take digital copies to share if they are special events showing a lot of family members.

A New Life for Family Photos, Videos, and Slides

If a family member is particularly ambitious or crafty, a digital photo book of select photos would make a great Christmas present! Or frame a special photo for each family member as a special memento. Take digital photos of shots you feel ambiguous about. Then you can toss the paper original and still have the digital copy. No one will mind later getting a text with a picture of Reilly when she was just a puppy. We can't tell you how many jobs we have done where the last thing in the house is the family photos. Slides and videos (especially on older formats) are more difficult to review, so many families will just trash them. It's tough, but understandable. How many times are those photos looked at, anyway? You can always pay someone to digitize these items, but it isn't cheap.

Crafting Family History

That wonderful quilt Aunt Laura made...Is there a fashionista in the family who can turn it into a jacket? Or put colorful pieces into frames so that sisters can each have a memory of her? How about that china set no one wants? One of our clients repurposed some precious china pieces as jewelry. Or if someone loves unique furniture, use china fragments for a tile-like tabletop. Recently we found someone who makes bags from old military uniforms. There are so many ways to preserve and honor your precious memories without filling your attic and garage!

Letting go

Your Mom loved that Hummel so much, it reminded her of you. But Hummels aren't really your thing. It's okay to let it go. Again, you can snap a shot to have as a reminder. But please try to let go of the guilt as well!

Honoring the past

If no one in the family wants an item or collection, consider donating it for a good cause. Or gifting it to a family friend as a memory of your loved one. After our mother passed, we gave pieces from our mother's rose glass collection to family and friends, and they were extremely touched to have that bit of reminder of her.

Monetary Value

A wonderful set of modern Swedish silverware, a Stickley dresser, a diamond tennis bracelet, a Mid-Century Modern coffee table…some household items will be desirable for what they are potentially worth, as well as for how they hold memories.

Appraisal

As mentioned earlier, when sorting items, some will stand out in value. You'll want to take gold and silver items, for instance, to someone who can let you know what they are worth, so family members can then decide whether to keep the items or sell them. When dealing with items of monetary value, it's important to keep track of who is receiving what value to ensure fairness and legality. Appraising every item can be expensive, but for some items, it's necessary. Where do we find heirlooms? Everywhere? Yes, possibly, but here are a few categories where they are most commonly found:

Artwork These items can be challenging. Unless it is a masterwork or holds significant historical importance, it's often best divided among family members based on personal preference. Less emotionally significant, yet still appealing pieces can be sold at an estate sale. Important pieces should be evaluated by an auction house, and the proceeds divided among the family.

Furniture Many families invested in furniture meant to be handed down, but unfortunately, most pieces haven't retained their value. However, rare or unique items, especially those with historical or regional appeal, can still hold significant worth. Consulting with an estate service can help identify potential treasures.

Antiques These pieces often hold both monetary and sentimental value. Families can choose to auction prized pieces, divide items among those with interest, or sell them online or to a dealer. These decisions are best made collectively, as once an item is gone, it's gone.

Jewelry Jewelry, especially pieces made of gold, silver, or gemstones, can hold significant value. It's worth having these appraised by a professional jeweler to determine their worth. Sentimental items like wedding rings or heirloom brooches may be best kept within the family, while less meaningful pieces can be sold.

Collectibles Collectibles such as coins, stamps, or vintage toys value will depend on the collection and condition. These items are best appraised by specialists in their respective fields to ensure an accurate valuation. Families can then decide whether to keep, sell, or donate them. Common collections such as figurines, Waterford crystal, LLadro, Hummels, and Fenton glass, have value depending on the piece and condition although, as mentioned before, they don't have as much value as they once did.

Books and Manuscripts Rare books, first editions, or manuscripts can be valuable. Have these evaluated by a rare book dealer or auction house if you suspect they may hold monetary worth. Otherwise, sentimental pieces can be distributed among family members who appreciate them.

Memorabilia Items like sports memorabilia, historical artifacts, or signed pieces can carry significant value. These should be carefully appraised and handled with care to ensure proper valuation and preservation.

By focusing on these key areas, you can ensure that family heirlooms are properly evaluated, appreciated, and distributed in a fair and meaningful way.

Handling Historical Items: A Guide to Downsizing with Care

When it comes to downsizing historical items, there are often two layers of significance to consider: family historical value and broader historical value. These items can be deeply sentimental, financially valuable, or even culturally significant. Here's a practical guide to help you decide the best course of action for these unique possessions.

Evaluate the Item

Before deciding what to do with a historical item, assess its value. This process can involve:

Family Value Does the item hold personal or familial importance? Examples might include handwritten letters, family Bibles, or heirloom jewelry.

Historical or Cultural Value Does the item have significance beyond your family? This could include antiques, documents, or artifacts tied to a specific time period, event, or community.

Financial Value Consult with a professional appraiser to understand the monetary worth of the item. This is especially important for high-value items like rare collectibles, art, or vintage furniture.

Once You Determine An Item Has Historical Value

Once you've evaluated the item, consider these options for downsizing:

Pass It Down to Family

Who Wants It? Communicate with family members to see if anyone is interested in keeping the item. Historical items often carry stories, making them meaningful to relatives.

Document the History Write down any known history of the item to pass along. This ensures the story doesn't get lost over generations.

Donate to a Museum or Historical Society

Research Relevance Find a museum, archive, or historical society that aligns with the item's significance. For instance, a Revolutionary-War-era musket might be ideal for a local history museum.

Get Tax Benefits Donations to nonprofit organizations can often provide tax deductions. Consult a tax professional to understand the benefits.

Preserve the Item Properly Museums are equipped to care for fragile or rare items, ensuring their longevity.

Sell the Item

Auction Houses High-value historical items, such as rare books or antiques, often fetch the best prices at specialized auction houses.

Online Marketplaces Websites like eBay, or Etsy, can connect you with buyers looking for unique items.

Private Collectors Contact collectors or dealers who specialize in your item's category.

Ethical Considerations Be cautious about selling items of cultural or historical importance that may be better preserved in a museum.

Preserve It Yourself

Storage Use archival-quality materials, such as acid-free boxes and sleeves, to protect sensitive items like photos, documents, or textiles.

Display Consider showcasing historical items in your home as part of your decor.

Communicate the Plan

For family items, clear communication is key. Avoid misunderstandings or disputes by:

Holding a Family Meeting Discuss your plans and invite feedback.

Creating a Written Record Document who receives what and why. This is especially helpful for future generations.

Special Considerations for Broader Historical Value

Some items may hold significant importance to a larger community, country, or even the world. For these:

Work with Experts Contact historians, archivists, or cultural organizations to determine the best course of action. This could include consulting local authorities.

Ensure Legal Compliance Make sure you're complying with laws related to the sale or export of artifacts. For example, some countries restrict the sale of items deemed cultural heritage. You can't easily sell items made from ivory. Some states do not allow it, there are strict rules as to what you can sell made from ivory. Do your homework.

Be Mindful of Ethics of Repatriation If the item originates from another country or culture, consider returning it to its rightful place.

Preserve the Stories & Embrace the History

Every historical item carries a story. Even if you decide to let go of it, you can make sure its story doesn't disappear by:

Digitizing Scan documents, photographs, or artwork to create a digital record.

Sharing Online Use platforms like StoryCorps or social media to document and share the history.

Creating a Memory Book Compile a scrapbook or digital book detailing the item's significance and journey.

Final Thoughts on Heirlooms

Downsizing historical items requires thoughtfulness and care, balancing emotional attachment with practical decisions. Whether you choose to pass an heirloom to family, donate it to a museum, or sell it to a collector, the key is ensuring its value, personal, cultural, or financial, is preserved. In doing so, you're not just parting with an object; you're ensuring its legacy lives on.

Wrapping Up Sort & Organize

Once you have completed sorting the heirlooms and the rest of the house or property, it's time for the fun part: distributing the contents. In most cases you have, by this point, thrown out a bunch of stuff, given some away, and set things aside.

You have put yourself and your team in a great position for the next phase. Review your plan and your charter. It's time to communicate with the family and let them know what's going on to close out the Sort & Organize phase. Here's a sample email:

Email 2: End of Sort & Organize Phase

Subject: Treasures found and next steps

Hello [Family Member/Team],

We've just wrapped up the sort and organize phase, and it's been quite an adventure! Along the way, we uncovered some hidden gems, Grampa's old Waltham pocket watch, tons of old coins, and a few thousand pieces of jewelry.

We will be doing further research on some of the items. I want to thank everyone for pitching in. Sorting through everything wasn't easy, but we made great progress together. Now, we're moving on to the Distribute phase—finding new homes for items that no longer fit our plans.

I have attached the list of the larger items and their planned homes. Let me know if you have any questions.

Let's keep the positive energy going!

Warm regards,

[Your Name]

In all your correspondence, keep it simple but most importantly...yes, we are about to lecture you...make sure the tone is family-friendly, (if the family is not friendly, use your imagination), hits the high points, doesn't insult anyone, and most importantly, communicates what was discovered, and the plans for the next phase.

Now, where does everything go?

GARAGE, KITCHEN & HOME OFFICE

The garage, kitchen, and home office are reported as the most cluttered spaces in the average home.

No surprise that many people find tackling these areas the most overwhelming!

Chapter 9
Phase 3: Distribute, What Goes Where

Letting Items Go, The Core of Downsizing

Distributing the contents of a home is often the most time-consuming and emotionally challenging phase of the downsizing process. This phase is where all your hard work in sorting and organizing comes to life. To recap, "distribute" means determining the final destination for each item: whether it's to be kept, sold, donated, recycled, trashed, or otherwise disposed of.

Before diving into the Distribute phase, let's clarify what the Sort & Organize phase did and didn't do. Sort & Organize is about identifying the major items that matter: the furniture, heirlooms, and high-value belongings that need decisions on whether to keep, donate, sell, or discard. (It's not about sorting through every single utensil in the kitchen drawer or meticulously organizing every pan in the cupboard. Small items and everyday clutter can often wait until later in the process, now is not the time.)

We focused first on the big-picture items that required more thought and family input. By keeping your attention on these larger decisions, you made meaningful progress without getting bogged down. Now it's time to let some things go.

In fact, you've already started this process by getting rid of the "junk" or useless items we discussed in Chapter 2. By clearing out those initial unnecessary items, you've made space, both physically and mentally, for the deeper work of distributing the more meaningful possessions. While it may feel daunting, tackling this step methodically ensures that every item is handled thoughtfully and with purpose. Even if you haven't started getting rid of stuff, let's dive into how to approach this critical phase with confidence and efficiency.

I (John) started one of our jobs, years ago in Raynham, Massachusetts with an amazing couple who were moving back to Illinois to be closer to their kids. They were getting older and needed to downsize. I was standing in the living room with the wife, a retired teacher. She stood with her hands on her face, just shaking her head.

"Look at all this stuff. How are we ever going to get rid of it, and move it, and sell it?" She said.

I said, *"Did you ever hear the old Chinese proverb?"*

She just looked at me with a quizzical look on her face. I knew it was quizzical because she was a teacher.

"No I haven't," she finally said.

"A journey of a thousand miles begins with a single step".

She smiled.

"Now, what do you want me to do with this figurine?" I asked, and off we went. How do you get the real work going efficiently and effectively? We'll go room

by room to give you an idea of the challenges and approaches to downsize each type. The good news is when you are downsizing (Downsizing To Go especially) is that everything must go.

Keep in mind the overall process of downsizing.

It's about making steady, thoughtful progress as you clear out the estate. The distribute phase is where decisions are made about who receives what, whether items are being kept, shared with family, or sent elsewhere. To keep things manageable, it's helpful to break it down room by room.

You can start in any room or area, but we prefer to begin with the bedrooms. Smaller bedrooms are typically easier to clear, and starting here gives you an immediate sense of accomplishment. These rooms often contain valuables, sentimental items, and personal belongings that should be set aside for family review. Clearing the bedrooms first creates extra space, a necessity during the downsizing process. Since bedrooms are usually tucked away, they make convenient in-house storage zones for temporarily holding items you've sorted or plan to distribute later.

Let's look at tackling the Master Bedroom. While this may be the last bedroom you clear, we'll use it as an example because it's usually the toughest bedroom to tackle. It's a significant part of the house and often holds both emotional and practical items. Decluttering or emptying this space marks significant progress. By accomplishing this, you'll set the tone for the rest of the downsizing journey and begin creating order, one space at a time. As an added bonus, the Master Bedroom, being larger, can be used to store and set aside important (moveable) family items during the downsizing process as we've done in many jobs.

When we clear out an estate, many times we will set aside one bedroom for the family items. Most things (that can be moved easily) are stored in the family bedroom during the downsizing to make sure important items are kept aside.

Bedrooms and Closets

Options for Clothes

Clearing out bedrooms can feel like a big task, but with the right approach, it's straightforward. But yes, you'll have to deal with clothes, and a lot of them. We always get asked about the best way to handle clothes for an estate. The answer is: it depends on the estate. During the Plan phase or even in Sort & Organize phase we decide on the overall approach for the clothes. Once you've separated items that will not be kept, there are several ways to get rid of unwanted clothes - each with its own pros and cons. Here are the most common options:

Donating is one of the easiest ways to go, as it helps those in need and might even give you a tax deduction. It's quick to drop off clothes at a charity, though the downside is you won't make any money from it, and some organizations might not take everything, especially if the items are worn out.

Selling If you're looking to make a little extra cash, selling your clothes online or through a garage sale is another route. While selling can bring in money, it can be time-consuming to list items, negotiate prices, and handle shipping. Garage sales are an option too, but you might not earn much for the effort you put in.

Consignment is where stores sell the clothes for you and give you a cut of the sale. This can be great for higher-end or gently used clothes, but stores can be picky and may reject items that don't fit their style or standards. Plus, you only get a percentage of the sale, and it could take a while for your clothes to sell.

Recycling For clothes that are too worn out to donate or sell, recycling is an eco-friendly choice. Some stores or textile recycling centers accept old fabrics, which helps keep clothes out of landfills. However, you'll need to find places that take these items, which can sometimes be a bit tricky.

Handing Down Lastly, handing down clothes to family or friends is a nice way to keep them in use, especially if certain items have sentimental value. The challenge is that not everyone may need or want the clothes, so you'll have to figure out who would like them.

Address Sentimental and High Value Items

Bedrooms are often home to sentimental and personal items like photos, letters, jewelry and memorabilia. This step requires extra time and care. During Sort & Organize you may have separated and labeled these items. Now its time to decide to keep, sell or let go

Jewelry If you haven't done so already in the last phase, set aside those costume or less-expensive pieces marked to sell for your yard or estate sale. Keep valuable jewelry in a safe, labeled place for sale or distribution to family members.

Photos Digitize as many as you feel you need to. Save some for family and friends. Shred others to protect privacy.

Maintain a Memory or Keepsake Area Box for items that remain undecided.

Decorative/Personal Items Decide with the family/team who will get important items such as handmade quilts and the like.

Clearing out a master bedroom can be an emotional process, especially when it's tied to years of memories. But letting go of items that no longer worn can be freeing.

The Kitchen: It's Not As Intimating As It Looks

Kitchens can be intimidating but don't have to be. It's just volume, and most can be donated or trashed. Save useful items for the family and to sell. If selling, it's best to group items in order to get enough value to interest buyers. One spatula isn't going to do it!

During Sort & Organize you got a picture of what's in the kitchen that's important. Now it's time to distribute the contents. Here's a list of kitchen item categories and what you can do with the items in each category.

Categories of Kitchen Items		
	WHAT TO DO	**COMMENTS**
COOKWARE AND BAKEWARE	Keep or sell "good" brands. Donate used. Dispose of overly used.	Good pots and pans as well as some retro bakeware have selling value.
GADGETS & UTENSILS	Sets may have value. If selling, best to group items.	Nice sets will sell, but don't expect much. Mismatched items best for donation.
DINNERWARE, GLASSWARE, FLATWARE	Keep or sell reputable sets. Donate used but good conditions.	Brands people know will sell, but probably for less than you think.
SMALL APPLIANCES	Items that often sell (condition dependent: blenders, food processors, mixers, toasters, microwaves, coffee makers, slow cookers, air fryers, specialty items.	Dispose of any items that have questionable electrical connections or are in otherwise bad condition.
MISC. ITEMS Food storage, containers, cleaning products	Keep storage items in good shape for selling or donating. Toss overly used/in bad condition.	Usually not a lot of value, but many items are good to donate. Keep the cleaning products for use at the end of downsizing.
FOOD	Donate or keep items that are good. Toss expired.	A fridge full of food gone bad is horrible to deal with. Get to it immediately.
COOKBOOKS	Check for vintage or old books. Some are valuable.	Donate most.
HOLIDAY ITEMS	Sell known brands which can still bring a good price.	Donate "normal" holiday items. Keep or sell the rest.

By now you've emptied those cabinets and drawers. (But did you empty all of them?) You might have been surprised to find items like a fondue set someone got as a gift and never used. You asked yourself *"Do I really need 12 spatulas?"* (Answer: probably not.)

Living Room: Creating a Cozy, Clutter-Free Space

Next, let's head to the living room, where most people spend a lot of their time. Start with your organized pile of big volume items such as electronics, DVDs, CDs, VHS, and books. If you're questioning that stack of DVDs that you haven't watched years, it might be time to let them go. As for VHS or cassette tapes, there is not a lot of demand (not even for Disney Black Diamond), so it's best to donate or dispose of them.

Then, tackle the other stuff in your undecided piles: décor items, throw pillows, and that mysterious pile of remote controls. Always keep an area to collect cords, remotes, and small electronics so you can match them up later or dispose of the them at the local electronics recycling center. Most small electronics are outdated and worthless (or close) but some still have value. Keep only what makes you happy or serves a purpose. If you're holding onto magazines from 2005 "just in case," it's time to recycle. And all that JFK memorabilia that all our parents or grandparents have? No need to save it.

Bathrooms: Toss It Out

The bathroom might be small, but it's mighty when it comes to clutter. Go through the toiletries and toss anything expired. Keep only the products that are used and loved. Some items can be donated but most used items should be tossed.

For the medicine cabinet, remember to dispose of old medications properly. And if your towels are more "scratching post" than "spa day," consider upgrading and donating the old ones to an animal shelter.

Attics & Basements: Tackling the Toughest Spaces

Ah, the attic and basement, the final frontiers of downsizing. These spaces are where old furniture, holiday decorations, and mystery boxes go to hide. For basements and attics it's always a good approach to get a volunteer team, usually two people, for the job. Let them go at it.

Your first step in the Sort & Organize phase was to get rid of the obvious junk. Then you assessed any items of potential value. Now it's time to dig deeper and make some decisions.

For this phase you may need a family member on hand (if you are using outside help) to decide on some select items. Remember, don't let the dust and dirt fool you - there could be some items of real value - either for the family history or for your wallet. If there are questions on something, have them put the item aside.

> **Attics** usually contain a lot of items that can be grouped for Garage or Estate Sales such as holiday items, old clothing, artwork etc.

> **Basements** often contain old and sometimes inherited furniture, vintage tools and a toy railroad or two. So be sure to peek under the dust for treasures. And, of course, there will be more holiday items.

Sheds/Barns:

An outbuilding can be an intimidating mess of items at first. But once you've cleared the shed/barn/garage of items that clearly have no value, it starts to be clearer what has value and what doesn't. If you've been through sorting and organizing already, here are the next steps:

> **Bring a trash and recycling bin close to the shed**, as well as several heavy-duty super-size trash bags. If possible, clear a dry, flat area near the shed and take out all the items you can.

> **Dispose of old paint and other liquids** (please see local guidelines and/or refer to Appendix).

> **Cart away your separated trash and recycling** (if you haven't done so already).

> **Set aside anything of value** (larger items such as lawn mowers, yard

equipment, tractors, etc. as well as tools and other still-useful items.)

Put back items that need to be protected from weather and that will be sold or donated.

Garages: Our Favorite Storage Location

Hopefully by this time you've sorted out the garage and have a wide open, covered and secure space for all the boxes and bins you've been putting the contents of your house into.

Imagine clearing a shelf of knick-knacks into a donation box and storing it in a stack of donation boxes, all organized in the garage. Isn't that a nice picture?

The challenge, however, is clearing out the garage itself—a task that can be overwhelming and, let's be honest, sometimes unpleasant. Here's how to tackle it effectively:

Start With a Quick Scan You've stared at that crowded garage a thousand times, but now it's time to clear it. First, identify large, obvious items that can be dealt with immediately, like old furniture, broken tools, or empty boxes. These can often go straight to the trash or recycling. Typically, there are many unused and outdated items that can be thrown away immediately.

Divide and Conquer Break the garage into zones. Yes, even if it's a small garage you can still think of it in zones. For example, focus on one corner or section at a time. This prevents the feeling of being overwhelmed by the sheer volume of items.

Organize Into Categories As you work, sort items into clear categories: Keep, Donate, Trash, Recycle. Use sturdy bins or boxes to keep everything organized. The categories for garages tend to be: car-related items, home upkeep, lawn care, tools, paint, cleaning products, and outdoor holiday décor.

Dispose of Hazardous Materials Many garages contain items like old paint, chemicals, or batteries. These require special handling and should be taken to a local hazardous waste disposal facility (not as easy as it sounds). Latex paint can be tossed if dried out.

Check for Valuables Garages often hold forgotten treasures, like tools, sports equipment, or collectibles. Set these aside for family review or potential sale.

Clean as You Go Once a section is cleared, sweep or vacuum the area to keep things tidy. We like to clean each area after it's clear. Not a deep clean, but it will look and feel better once an area is cleared. This also makes it easier to use the garage as a staging area for the downsizing process.

Set Up Temporary Zones Once the garage is cleared, designate specific areas for items destined for donation, recycling, trash, or family review. Label these zones clearly to keep everyone on the same page.

Clear Frequently Don't let the piles of trash or donation items get too large. Make frequent trash and donation runs during the job, even if it's just a bag or two at a time.

By clearing and organizing the garage early in the downsizing process, you create a functional space that simplifies the rest of the project. It becomes your central hub for sorting and staging items, making the entire downsizing journey smoother and more efficient.

For many downsizing projects, the distribution phase naturally leads to decisions about selling items. Whether it's family heirlooms, furniture, or collectibles, finding the right method to sell these items is an important part of the process.

The most popular option is an estate sale, but there are other methods that might suit your needs better, such as online marketplaces, auctions, or consignment. The key is to choose the method that works best for your timeline, goals, budget and the quality of items you are open to selling.

In the next two chapters, we'll dive deeper into the world of selling items. We'll explore the different methods available, share tips for maximizing value, and guide you through hosting a successful estate sale. Of course you'd like to know how to make the most of your family's treasures. In the meantime, congratulate yourselves on getting to the heart of downsizing. Pat yourselves on the back for all your hard work!

Now let's see how you can get some return on your investment.

Chapter 10
Phase 3: Turning Items Into Cash

$elling Your Items

Selling Items: A Guide

One of the more challenging aspects of the Distribute phase is determining the value of items and deciding what can be sold and how. Now that you and your team have sorted the home's contents into categories, it's time to review the items you labeled and agreed to sell in the Sort & Organize phase. Let's explore getting value out of those items.

Review Identified Sellable Items

Take another look at your "sell" items and figure out what's truly worth selling. Ask yourself the following questions:

Is it in good condition?
Is it something people still want or need?
Do you think it has value?
Will it likely be easy to sell?

Determining what is sellable or not requires a balance of practicality and market awareness. Start by evaluating the condition of each item. Damaged, incomplete, or heavily worn items are generally not worth trying to sell, as buyers expect quality and usability. Items in excellent or good condition stand a much better chance of attracting interest. Check current estate sales in your area online to see what's attracting buyers, what's really selling and for how much.

Next, think about demand. Just because something is useful doesn't mean it's desirable. Focus on items that align with current trends or have timeless appeal. Currently, furniture with clean lines or mid-century modern design tends to sell well, for example. Traditional brown furniture, while popular in the past, is less desirable now.

What about collectibles? We have downsized dozens of collections including trains, Hummels, Waterford crystal, decorative plates, Lladro, Fenton glass, tools, Byers Carolers, pewter, art, and more. Sometimes, estates with large collections warrant multiple or dedicated sales. For example, a massive train collection may be sold in its own estate sale, while the remaining household items are handled separately.

Imagine walking into the home of a couple in their 80s. You might find:

- Hummels
- Lladro figurines
- German beer steins
- Decorative plates
- Knick-knacks from around the world
- Byer's Carolers

- Baseball cards
- Stamp collections
- VHS tapes

What in this list has retained its value? Unfortunately, not much.

Why Is That?

It all comes down to supply and demand. Tastes change, and so does the market for collectibles. Items highly coveted decades ago, like decorative plates or Hummels, often have little-to-no demand today. Their value is low or nonexistent, and in some cases, you might even have to pay to get rid of them.

This reality is crucial when making final decisions about items. For instance, a large collection of Norman Rockwell plates is better off being donated than added to a sale. Similarly, most baseball cards, comic books, and stamps don't have much value. Our advice when checking sales prices is to use a website that shows actual "sold for" prices, not just listed prices.

Choosing the DIY Approach-Options

Online Marketplaces Platforms like eBay, Facebook Marketplace, and Craigslist help you sell items locally or nationwide. Large items like furniture or electronics are ideal for local pickup. Clothes and jewelry can be shipped easily.

Garage/Yard Sales These let you offload many items quickly. While profits are typically low, yard sales offer community engagement and quick results.

Consignment Shops Though technically an outside service, you will have to bring your items and agree on a sales price. Typically, you receive 50% of the shop's sale price. Research local shops, confirm what they'll accept, and agree on terms in writing. Be aware that items may not sell within the timeframe, and you may need to retrieve unsold goods.

DIY Tips – For both Garage/Yard Sales and Online Sales

Price Your Items Right Research similar items online to understand market value. Remember, buyers won't pay full price for used items, so be prepared to offer fair deals. Garage sales should have low prices to move items quickly.

Be Safe and Smart Meet buyers in public places to exchange items. Avoid sharing personal details. Accept secure payments like cash, PayPal, or Venmo.

DIY Tips – For Online Sales, *Get Ready to Sell!*

Clean your items Dust, wash, and repair items to make them presentable.

Take clear photos High-quality pictures help items stand out online.

Write honest descriptions Include condition, size, and key details. If the item has anything wrong with it make sure it's included in the description.

Be patient. Selling takes time. If something doesn't sell right away, try lowering the price or bundling it with other items. The goal is to clear space and give your items a new life.

By following these steps, you can sell items effectively on your own and put extra cash in your pocket while downsizing.

Considering an Estate Sale with A Service

While yard sales and Facebook Marketplace can help you clear some of your less important clutter, we find for most families an estate sale is the best option. Let's explore how to hold an estate sale, what to sell, and what to avoid selling.

Estate Sales

If you're downsizing a lot of items, have family in another state, or are on a tight timeline, hiring an estate sale service can make the process easier. While they charge a fee, they handle organizing and selling on your behalf.

Most of the time, downsizing is the solution to an immediate need, so outside estate sale services are often called upon to help sort out and dispense a home's contents quickly and more easily. The estate sale is the most popular method to sell large numbers of items. There are several reasons for the popularity of estate sales: much of the work is done by others; the process can be much quicker than if you were doing it on your own: and you may achieve a higher return than from your own yard/garage/picker sale.

How is an Estate Sale Different Than a Yard Sale?

An estate sale is a comprehensive process of selling the majority of a home's contents, typically after a downsizing, move, or the passing of a loved one. A yard sale focuses on clearing out a limited number of unwanted items.

An estate sale involves a more organized approach to selling a wide range of items, from furniture and collectibles to everyday household goods. The goal is to maximize value while finding new homes for most of the home's belongings, except for those items that family members wish to keep. The best part, you can do it all at once! Yes, you can try to do this yourself, but so much work will be lifted from your shoulders if you invest in an estate sale service. And then you won't have to worry about all the additional details like shipping, organizing for the sale, price-tagging, online listings, etc.

An estate sale includes everything a family (and/or service) thinks will have some value. Furniture, kitchen items, décor items, antiques, tools, clothing, collectibles...basically everything that is saleable. The sale should only occur after you have sorted through the house or property and identified (more importantly, removed) the items that the family members/friends want. Once that's done, everything else can be sold at the estate sale.

In-Person vs. Online Auctions

There are pluses and minuses for each way to go. The traditional method has been an in-person auction/estate sale vs. one that is online. (In this book, we won't go into Auction Houses, but please note that they will only take items they believe have monetary value and will take about 10-30% or more of the earnings. Auction houses are great for selling some specific high value items, but they are not the way to empty an estate.)

With so much business on the web now, online auctions/sales have become much more popular. Let's discuss both in-person and online, how you can assess what's right for you, and what you can expect.

In-Person Estate Sale

An in-person estate sale may have unexpected extra costs, depending on who you hire. If the sale is taking place within the home, security and/or personnel in each room are cost factors. Parking will have to be considered and arranged. Neighbors may have to be informed if you expect many buyers. Nonetheless, the advantages of an in-person estate sale are:

> **Viewing & Immediate Transaction** Buyers can physically examine items before purchasing. They can make on-the-spot purchases, leading to quick sales and cash flow for the seller. Plus, buyers can take items home immediately, avoiding the need for shipping or delivery arrangements. Additionally, they can make their own furniture pickups. And although preparation may be lengthy, once the sale is done, cleanout can happen immediately.
>
> **Price Negotiation** If a potential buyer feels the listed price is too high, a new price can be negotiated on the spot.

In-person sales can also have drawbacks. For one, hired services that specialize in in-person sales often cherry pick only high-value items, leaving you with a lot left to deal with. And the audience is basically local. To mention a few negatives:

Limited Audience Fewer eyes mean fewer buys. Even if advertised, people will only travel so far and out-of-state buyers are extremely unlikely.

Weather and Bad Timing In-person sales are vulnerable to external factors like bad weather, which can significantly reduce attendance. Additionally, scheduling the sale near holidays or during big events can cause low turnout.

Lack of Privacy If you are sensitive to the idea of people roaming through your home and picking through your family's things, then this sort of sale should be avoided.

Online Estate Sale/Auction

Online sales have the advantage of potentially drawing a larger audience, and certainly do not require large numbers of people poring through your home and family history. You may hire a service to do a sale online, in which case fixed prices are assigned or to create an auction, where people can bid against each other, driving up prices. You will still have to deal with parking on pickup day, but pickups can be spaced out and scheduled. Here are some advantages to selling online:

Wider Audience to Reach More Buyers Online estate sales allow you to connect with people beyond your local area. This can result in more potential buyers, especially for unique or valuable items. With a little targeting word-of-mouth or advertising you can attract collectors who may live far away to collectible items in the estate.

Safer, Cleaner With an online estate sale, you avoid having crowds of people coming into your home. This can be especially important if you're concerned about security or health issues. And, because payments are handled online, risks associated with cash interactions or dealing with scams or actual thieves are reduced.

Less Stressful for the Seller You won't need to host or manage the logistics of having strangers in your home or answer questions in real time. You can have everything set up online and monitor the sale at your convenience. Selling online allows you to take your time setting up and listing items, without the rush of a one-day or weekend event. You can post items gradually, reducing the pressure to get everything done quickly.

Better Tracking and Organization Many online platforms automatically create an inventory of your items as you list them, making it easy to track what's sold and what's still available. Online platforms often provide clear documentation of sales, making it easier to track payments and manage finances.

Flexible Timing Unlike in-person estate sales that typically last for one or two days, online estate sales can run for a longer period, giving more people a chance to buy. And with an online sale, you won't have to worry about bad weather affecting attendance. Rain or shine, the sale can continue without problems.

Online estate sales can be a great way to simplify the process, attract more buyers, and reduce the stress involved in selling items from an estate.

An online sale doesn't have the same boundaries, so your audience can be anywhere in the country, provided you are okay with items being shipped. There's no real downside but note that the process may take a little longer.

Whether you choose online or in-person, it's often helpful to hire an outside service to relieve some of the burden. Please know that they will require a fee, and that each company has their own pricing method. A little research will help you find a reputable company. Of course, if you're in our neighborhood, we'd love to help!

How to Hold an Estate Sale

So how do begin to think about setting up an estate sale? And what should you look for in a company to help you run it? And most importantly, how do you make sure people see it?

The Harsh Reality of Estate Sales

There is a reason why companies charge a minimum for having an estate sale: it costs them money to set up and run the sale. Companies may make decisions on what they think will sell; they probably won't want to consider a collection of cut-glass items, for instance.

An Estate Sale is just that–A SALE! Think about what attracts you to buy an item. Is it unique, that color that you love or something that fits in that corner… For promotion, you will need something special to be the key item or collection to attract eyes to your sale. It probably won't be the sofa that someone paid $3,000 for. But it may be that retro mid-century-modern dishware or handsome pair of dog andirons.

Hire an Estate Sale Company or DIY with an Online Platform?

While you can run an estate sale by yourself, it's much easier to hire a professional company to do it for you. They'll organize everything, price your items, and manage the sale on the day of the event. Here's how to find the right company:

> **Do Your Research** Start by asking friends or family if they know any good estate sale companies. You can also look online for reviews and ratings. Check out websites like EstateSales.net or EstateSales.org or Facebook groups where people recommend companies.
>
> **Interview a Few Companies** Don't just go with the first company you find. Talk to at least two or three companies. Ask them how they work, what they charge, and how long they think it will take. They should

come to your house to see what you're selling before giving you an estimate. Listen to what they stand for: for example, if the company only does estate sales, then their focus will be on what valuable items you have available to sell. On the other hand, a company whose focus is downsizing seniors (as well as having estate sales) will focus on the complete picture. They'll have more of a family-friendly view since their revenue is not from estate sales alone.

Ask for References A good company will have past clients who can tell you about their experience. Ask for references and call them to see if they were happy with the service. Current online reviews are good too. The key is current reviews, actual reviews (not some canned made-up review some sites have).

What to Look for in an Estate Sale Company

If you are basing your decision on a company that promises to get you full/near-full value for items, beware! To be honest, the value of most items in a house/property will not come close what was initially paid. That being said, there are companies that get better results than other companies. How do they do it?

Their service area The area they service has bigger and more expensive properties which usually means more expensive stuff to put in an estate sale.

Their list They have their own email list and existing customers that buy from them.

Their marketing They emphasize the importance of marketing the sale. (We'll talk about marketing a little later but it's so important. Getting eyes on the sale or people to the sale is key.)

Their professionalism They provide professional services. What does that mean? If it's online, the sale and pictures look good, the lots make sense, and there are good descriptions on both the sale and individual items. They are organized and courteous.

What Are the Qualities of a Good Company?

Experience Look for a company that has been doing estate sales for a while. They'll know how to price items, attract buyers, and handle any issues that come up.

Transparency The company should be clear about their fees. Most estate sale companies take a percentage of what you make. Make sure they explain how their fee works and if there are any other costs (like advertising, pickup or minimums).

Professionalism You want a company that will treat your belongings with respect. They should organize the sale neatly and make sure everything is priced fairly. They should also be friendly and helpful to buyers during the sale. The online sale items should look good, have thorough descriptions, and be well advertised.

Marketing Skills Yes, we'll repeat the importance of marketing in estate sales. A good estate sale company knows how to attract buyers. They should take good photos, list the sale on estate sale websites, and use social media to get the word out.

What Shouldn't Be Sold at an Estate Sale?

The estate sale will include almost everything left in the house after you've taken what you want. However, some types of items are generally prohibited such as:

- Firearms (must be licensed)
- Alcohol (must be licensed)
- Counterfeit items (e.g. Fake Rolex Watches)
- Hazardous Materials

- Prescription Medications
- Stolen Goods
- Recalled Items
- Certain Wildlife or Animal Products
- Fireworks or Explosives (check state and local laws)
- Vehicles Without Proper Paperwork

It's important to check local and state laws when organizing an estate sale to avoid selling prohibited or regulated items. When in doubt, consult an estate sale professional or attorney to ensure compliance. Everything else is fair game for the sale. Make sure you have something enticing. So how do you attract buyers to your sale?

The Impact of Low-Value Items on Your Estate Sale

Including less-desirable items (aka "junk" or yard sale items) in an estate sale can hurt the sale. Cluttering the sale with low-value or unpopular items detracts from its overall success and makes it harder to attract serious buyers. In the estate sale business, we say, "more eyes, more buys." Junk items take attention away from high-value items and may turn people away.

Use Chapter 2 as a guide for what items may be valuable. While collectibles can be sold, temper expectations. Most won't fetch high prices. On rare occasions some pieces might surprise you.

Focus on quality over quantity Curate your sale to include in-demand items.

Donate or give away low-value items This clears space and ensures the sale remains focused on attractive, higher-value items.

Be realistic Just because an item was treasured in the past doesn't mean it holds the same value now.

By setting aside items with little demand and focusing on those with real potential, you'll ensure your estate sale is successful.

How to Attract Buyers

One of the most important parts of a successful estate sale is getting people to see your sale. Here's how you can attract more buyers:

Have a Featured Item to Attract More Eyes Have an item, usually a relatively expensive one, to catch people's attention and make them want to come to your sale. You can always put a reserve price on it, but it will get you more views. This could be a valuable or high-demand item like a car, riding lawn mower, rare collectibles, or high-end furniture. Advertise these items in your marketing to draw people in.

Advertise Online The estate sale company will usually post your sale on websites like EstateSales.net, but you can also help spread the word. Share the sale on your personal social media and ask friends or family to share it. Include photos of the items and make sure you highlight any special or valuable pieces.

Signs and Flyers For in-person estate sales, go old school! Put up signs around the neighborhood directing people to your sale. Make bright, clear signs with arrows that are easy for people to follow. You can also make flyers and post them in local coffee shops, grocery stores, or community centers. Again, send the sale info to friends and family. (They'll be good for a few sales.)

How the Sale Works In-Person

For in-person estate sales, on the day of the sale, the estate sale company will usually take care of everything. They'll set up the items, mark prices, and handle the money. Here's what happens:

The Setup The company will organize the items for sale throughout the house. Buyers will walk from room to room, looking at items and choosing what they want.

Pricing The company will price items based on their experience and the local market. They'll make sure prices are fair and encourage sales.

Running the Sale The company's staff will be there to answer questions, negotiate with buyers, and make sure everything runs smoothly.

How the Sale Works Online

For online estate sales, everything is photographed and catalogued on an estate sale platform. We use CTBids.com, but there are others available. Here's how it happens:

An online estate sale, such as those conducted on CTBids.com, works by listing items from an estate directly on an auction-style platform, where interested buyers can browse, bid, and purchase items. The process typically starts with creating a catalog of available items, including detailed descriptions and photographs. Buyers then place bids during a set time frame, and at the end of the auction, the highest bidder wins the item. The sale is organized with scheduled pickup times for buyers to collect their items from the estate, ensuring an efficient and organized transfer of goods. This approach allows a wider audience to participate in purchasing estate items, providing a streamlined way to manage downsizing or estate liquidation.

The Starting Bid of $1

OK, it may seem a little odd that many online estate sales start their bids at $1. It's our most-asked question when talking to a prospect about cleaning out their own or their relatives' estate. The conversation usually goes something like this:

> John; *"We start all bids, except the ones we don't want to, at one dollar."*

> Client: *"What! You going to sell my china cabinet for a $1?"*
>
> John: *"No, actually your china cabinet is not going to sell. And you'll have to pay to get rid of it."* OK, to be honest, I just think this. It's true, but It's better to break the news gently, so I explain to them something like the following.: *"The market for china cabinets is not great, since not many people use china or fancy dishes and glasses anymore. Most likely, no-one will buy it, and we will have to find it a home some other way."* (The other way is to give it away or sell it for a few bucks since it must be removed.)

Estate sale companies often start their bids at $1 for several strategic reasons, especially for online auctions. Here are some key motivations behind this practice:

To Generate Interest and Increase Participation A $1 starting bid creates a lower barrier to entry and encourages more people to participate because it presents a low-risk opportunity to place a bid. Buyers are more likely to engage if they feel they can get a bargain. More bidders mean more competition: By starting at $1, companies can increase the number of interested bidders, which typically drives up competition. More competition often results in higher final bids. For online sales, most of the activity happens in the last couple of days.

For The Psychological Effect It creates excitement. Starting at $1 can create excitement among potential buyers, as they perceive the opportunity to get a great deal. This sense of urgency and excitement can lead to a bidding war, pushing up the price much higher than it might have if it started closer to market value.

To Ensure Items Are Sold Lower, enticing prices encourage purchase, which helps you clear everything out.

To Let the Market (or in This Case the Sale) Drive the Price Starting at $1 allows the market to determine the true value of an item. Estate sale companies may not always know the exact market value of every item, and letting buyers bid up from $1 means the item will probably reach its fair market value.

To Eliminate Tough Decisions on Pricing Pricing hundreds of items individually can be time-consuming and risky. Starting at $1 is a straightforward strategy that avoids the risk of overpricing and discouraging bids.

To Achieve Higher Overall Sale Prices Through Competition The $1 starting bid can spark a bidding war between buyers, ultimately driving the final price above what the item would have sold for with a higher starting price. The excitement of outbidding someone else many times leads buyers to spend more than they originally intended.

To Get Higher Prices Ultimately The $1 bid has a cumulative effect: For an estate sale with many items, even if individual items sell for slightly less than expected, the increased number of participants and the excitement around bidding can lead to higher overall sales.

To Attract a Broader Audience Many buyers are attracted to auctions with low starting bids, as they hope to find great deals. A larger audience means a greater chance of achieving higher final bids, and it also creates a positive reputation for the estate sale company as one that provides value.

To Engage Bargain Hunters Starting bids at $1 draws in bargain hunters who might not otherwise be interested in higher-priced auctions. Even if they start with low bids, these participants can drive up competition as they become invested in the process.

Running the Sale:
Don't Panic, Nothing Happens on the First Day (or Week):

Depends on the company but many of the companies that run estate sales run them for 10 days or so (it does vary by company and sale). We tend to run our estate sales for 10 days. Nothing much happens in the first week when bidders are marking their lots and watching. The last three days is where all the action occurs.

What Happens After the Sale?

Once the sale is over, you can donate leftover items and do the cleanout. (The estate sale company will usually offer to help with any leftover items but ask in advance.) Many companies will arrange for leftover items to be donated to charity, but usually there is a lot more to clean out, especially if you want to responsibly re-cycle and re-use. A reputable company will usually take care of the end-game nitty-gritty.

So, Should You Do It?

Having an estate sale can be a great way to make money while downsizing your home. By hiring the right company, choosing the best time, and attracting buyers with valuable items, you'll have a successful sale. Just remember to plan ahead, pick an item to highlight the sale if you can and let the professionals handle the details!

By starting bids at $1, running the sale for 10 days, having a broad audience to reach bidders, estate sale companies effectively attract more participants, increase competition, and ensure that all items are sold, making it a highly successful strategy for many estate auctions. This approach also minimizes the risk of items being overpriced or left unsold, helping the company meet the primary goal of clearing out the estate efficiently. Yes, some of your stuff will go for $1 and that's the stuff that deserves to go for a $1. It's OK, let it go.

The End of the Distribute Step

You did it, a huge milestone in your downsizing journey! This is the home stretch, where most of the contents are finally distributed, and you can start seeing the light at the end of the tunnel. Whether you've donated, sold, or given items to family, it was all about finding a new home for these belongings and wrapping up the bulk of the work.

Now stay positive and keep your energy up for the final phase. You're almost there!

Wrapping Up the Distribute Phase

Communicate with the team on the progress they have made. Here's a sample email to communicate progress on the Distribute Phase.

Email 3: Distribute Phase is Done!

> **Subject:** Distribution complete—Here's where we stand
>
> Hello [Family Member/Team],
>
> We've officially completed the distribution phase, and I'm thrilled with how smoothly everything went! Many items have found happy new homes, and we've received some funds from the estate sale.
>
> I appreciate everyone's help and patience as we worked through finding the right place for everything. Next up, we tackle the final fix and cleanout—nearly there!
>
> Thanks again for being a wonderful team!
>
> Warm regards,
>
> [Your Name]

Now it's time to tackle the final touches like finishing those last fixes, making safety improvements, and completing any remaining repairs. And, of course, getting the rest of the stuff out!

At this stage, the estate looks good, but not quite great yet. It may still feel like there are too many things, but don't worry, this is the 'toss-the-rest' phase. Typically, this means letting go of anything that's left over after you've combed through the house 80 times.

The hard work is done, and now it's time for the final cleanout. Even though you have removed a mountain of items, what you will see in this phase, usually, is that each room or area of the house still has some stuff in it. It could be donation items, trash, old paint or hazardous waste. It all adds up. Meaning a little stuff from each area adds up to a lot of stuff. But don't get discouraged. It will be easy to get rid of.

Let's get ready for one last push.

Chapter 11
Phase 4: Fix & Final Cleanout

The final phase of your downsizing journey is all about getting your space ready for whatever comes next. Whether you're preparing a property for sale, ensuring a clean and safe living environment for continued occupancy, or simply removing the last remnants of clutter, this phase is crucial for tying up all the loose ends. It's not just about emptying the property. It's about creating a space that's functional, safe, and ready for its next chapter.

The difference between when you start the downsizing effort and when you finish it will amaze (or at least surprise) you in a good way. You're at the final step, what's left?

The Fix & Final Cleanout phase focuses on two key goals: removing the last items and making necessary repairs or upgrades. This can mean different things depending on your downsizing objective:

For Downsizing To Go (Complete Cleanout) Removing every last item so the property is fully empty and ready for sale, rental, or a new occupant.

For Downsizing To Stay (Decluttering and Safety) Decluttering and adding measures to make the space safer and more comfortable for the current occupants, especially if the goal is to age in place or create a more accessible environment for your loved ones.

Removing the Last Items

At this point, anything remaining in the estate is the hardest, toughest, nastiest stuff to remove. It's usually a bunch of random stuff, such as rusted cars or tractors, old boats, pianos, player pianos, organs (not the human kind), old wood, falling-apart wood sheds, oil burners that looked like they came from a real haunted house…that kind of stuff.

You've identified them and how to get rid of them in the prior phases, now it's time to execute.

Small Fixes and Repairs

During the Plan phase you identified the fixes and repairs for the project. Once the property has been emptied or significantly decluttered, it's time to make any necessary small fixes or repairs. The goal here is to do the necessary fixes i.e. the ones that make sense but don't break the bank. Here are some of the most common types of fixes during this phase:

Patch and Paint Painting wall and ceilings, repairing holes in walls and repainting can make a significant difference in how clean and updated the property feels.

Repairs Fixing broken windows or doors, replacing damaged carpet, or refinishing hardwood floors can improve both safety and aesthetics.

> **Remodeling** Do the small remodel enhancements to make the property safer to live or more attractive to buy.

Safety Upgrades for Aging in Place

If the goal is to make the property safe for aging in place, it's time to do the specific safety upgrades you identified in the planning phase. A few small upgrades can make a world of difference.

Here's a few things to consider when aging in place. We will take a room by room look; different rooms have different requirements.

> **Living rooms** Clear paths, get lift chairs or other senior-friendly furniture, fasten bookcases to the wall, and install handrails
>
> **Kitchen** Make sure that necessary items are accessible (not in high cabinets), countertops are clear of hazards, appliances are in working order, and any dangerous devices are removed.
>
> **Bedrooms** Put risers on beds, clear floor space around the room, have good night lighting and have essentials within reach, like butterscotch candies!
>
> **Bathroom** Include a higher toilet seat, grab bars, transfer benches for shower and bath (or add a walk-in tub), and have personal care products accessible.
>
> **Garages, Basements, and Attics** Clear them and leave as little as possible.
>
> **Technology** Evaluate the current technology offerings for senior safety. Technology such as easy-to-use cellphones, Alexa-like devices, smart devices to control lights and appliances. There are a lot available today to help seniors.

Decluttering for Comfort and Safety

For those who plan to stay in the property, decluttering for comfort and safety is a key focus. This might mean removing tripping hazards, ensuring that pathways are clear, and making the home feel more open and manageable. Here are some specific actions to take:

> **Remove Excess Furniture** Reducing the number of furniture pieces can make a space feel larger and improve accessibility.

> **Organize Everyday Items** Ensure commonly used items are easily accessible to avoid the need for climbing or bending.

> **Eliminate Tripping Hazards** Secure or remove loose rugs and ensure electrical cords are out of the way.

Bringing It All Together

The Fix & Final Cleanout is about setting the stage for the next phase of the property's life. Whether the property is being sold, rented, or prepared for a loved one to continue living there, this phase provides closure to the downsizing effort. It's about creating a safe, functional, and welcoming environment that serves the next chapter—whether that's a new family moving in or a senior comfortably aging in place.

A Practical Checklist for the Fix & Final Cleanout

To make this phase as smooth as possible, here's a checklist to guide you through the Fix & Final Cleanout:

> **Remove Last Items**
>
> - Check attics, basements, garages, and other storage areas.
>
> - Decide on last items: sell, donate, recycle, or trash.

Complete Small Repairs

- Patch and paint walls.

- Repair or replace flooring as needed.

- Ensure all doors, windows, and locks are functioning.

Make Safety Upgrades (if staying in the home)

- Install grab bars and handrails.

- Upgrade bathroom for accessibility.

- Improve lighting throughout the home.

- Declutter for comfort and safety

- Remove excess furniture.

- Organize commonly used items for easy access.

- Secure or remove tripping hazards.

By following this process, the Fix & Final Cleanout can be a rewarding conclusion to the downsizing journey. It provides the satisfaction of a job well done and ensures that the property is ready for whatever comes next.

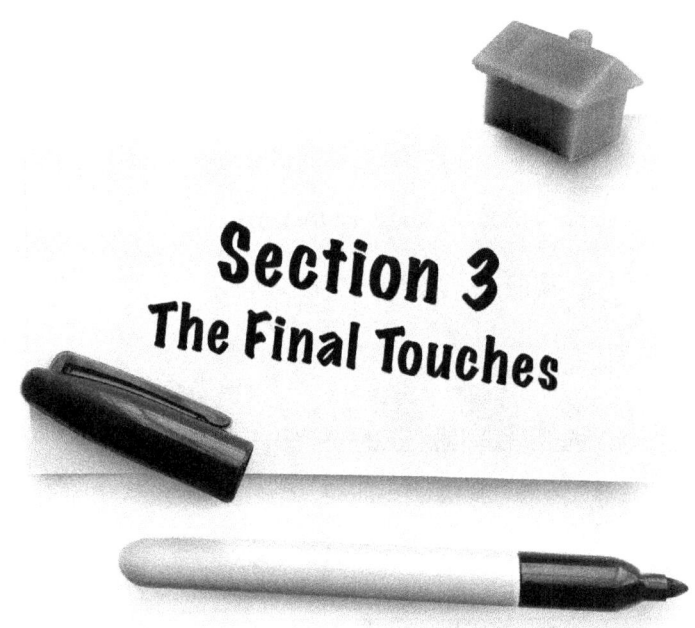

Section 3
The Final Touches

Chapter 12
The Tip Jar

Clean Out Tips and Techniques

Since we've been around this block a few times, we thought we'd pass on a few useful tips from things we've learned over the years. Some of these are from earlier chapters, but bear repeating.

TIP: Remember the 80/20 Rule

This little tidbit of info is known as The Pareto Principle: 80% of outcomes come from 20% of causes. This 80/20 rule can be a helpful guide when cleaning out houses and good to keep in the back of your mind as you are sorting and cleaning.

When it comes to value, here's how it works:

80% of Value Comes from 20% of Items

When selling or donating items during the downsizing process, you'll find that about 20% of your possessions hold 80% of the financial or sentimental value. Once these high-value items (heirlooms, artwork, valuable electronics) are handled, dealing with what remains becomes easier.

What else does that mean? That 80% of items will be easy to let go of! This especially applies to most everyday items, duplicates, or things that no longer serve a purpose.

When applied to cleaning out, here's how it works:

20% of Items Cause 80% of the Clutter

In most households, a small portion of items take up the most space. Like large, unused furniture, piles of clothing or magazines, excessive paperwork, or bulky items stored in basements or attics.

20% of the Home is Used 80% of the Time

People tend to use only a small portion of their home, such as the kitchen, bedroom, and living room. The rest of the house (basements, spare rooms, garages) may remain underused or completely unused. When downsizing, this observation helps prioritize what to keep. If certain rooms aren't contributing to daily life, chances are most of the items in them can be easily removed.

When talking about emotions, here's how it works:

80% of Stress Comes from 20% of Decisions

Downsizing often involves tough emotional decisions, and you may find that a few items cause the majority of the emotional stress. These might be sentimental items or family heirlooms. Knowing this can help you prepare for the emotional challenges and tackle them strategically, saving the easier decisions for later.

Here are some more tips we've gathered in our years of downsizing:

TIP: Don't Ignore the Junk Drawer. It's Manageable!
Do you have any idea on why it's called a junk drawer? (Of course you do, we are not trying to trick you just to share something that we have learned cleaning out hundreds of junk drawers.) 99.9999% of the time there is nothing, valuable in these drawers. Most often you will find screws, scissors, pens and pencils, scotch tape, batteries that may or may not work, and the like (everything except for the important papers everyone has been looking for). But, because there may be something important, you still must sort them.

Here's how you do it quickly:
Find an area and dump the drawer out. Or if you can't dump it, just start scooping it onto an area where you can spread everything out. Quickly separate items by type of item until the drawer is sorted. You'll have some piles to donate or trash or keep. Move them to the appropriate pile. Let it sit. When you go back to sort it one more time even more items will end up in the trash or donate pile.

TIP: Label Like Crazy
Labels are cheap. Post-it notes, tags, whatever means you want to use as a label, please use it! Labeling and tagging are easy to do and save a bunch of time, especially while sorting. How many times will you or someone from your team open the box of used Christmas cards in the corner of the closet? Label it once and you won't pick the same item up three times to wonder what's inside (Can you tell we speak from experience?).

TIP: Gather a Large Bunch of Boxes and Bags for Sorting

You're going to need some boxes and bags. Lots of them. The home may already have plastic bins, which are great for storing items you'll want to keep in areas such as garages, attics or closets. File cardboard boxes are great for paperwork and books and are a manageable size to pick up. Large cardboard boxes are useful for donations, and small boxes are great for sorted jewelry. Small sandwich and kitchen storage bags are great for sorting (and seeing!) jewelry and delicate scarves. And larger clear, white and black bags will be necessary. See earlier chapters for details.

Know at the end of the job you'll probably have a bunch left over. But better too many than too few!

TIP: Have a Large "Miscellaneous" Box Close At Hand

As you work, you will come across some items that you don't know what to do with. This can stop your progress dead. Instead of indecisively stopping, put the item in a "miscellaneous" box and move on. The box will end up containing worthless items which you will go through more quickly later. (I have them in most rooms or areas I clear.) Keep things moving along!

TIP: Create Zones

Especially if you know you have a lot of an item (books, CDs, collectibles, etc.) throughout the home, dedicate one or more areas where you can add to that "group". This is especially important for the "Where-the-heck- does-this-item-belong category." While it may seem counterintuitive to put it aside, in the end it will be faster for these two reasons:

• You don't waste time trying to figure out what to do with a giant paperclip. You put in aside with the other office items and move on.

• Most of time the stuff you put in the "aside" box or area is either donated or junked. On another note, you may find the missing issue of a valuable book set!

TIP: If you are having an estate sale, have something big to attract eyes
Feature something big (like a car or sit-down lawn mower) or valuable, rare or just plain attractive to draw interest in your sale. Set a reserve price to be sure you get at least that much. As far as a commission goes, negotiate a reduced commission (15–20%) for expensive items like cars.

TIP: Create Space–Make some room!
Start off by making some working space immediately. Pick a room or a spot, which you will probably have to clear. Usually, it will be an area that will end up having a large volume of items that will be donated or recycled or trashed from sneaky clutter spots such as closets, book shelves or offices.

TIP: Sort with Purpose
Consistently follow your system. Use a clear categorization system like "Keep," "Donate," "Sell," "Discard." Label boxes or bags clearly for each category. And handle each item once. Encourage your help to follow this "one touch" rule: make decisions quickly and avoid handling items multiple times. Pick it up, decide, and move on.

TIP: Work Collaboratively & Efficiently
Communicate with the team. Be patient and empathetic, as downsizing can be an emotional process. Clear communication on what to keep, sell, or donate is essential. Delegate specific roles (e.g., sorting, packing, removing items) to increase efficiency. Have a lead organizer and assign others to specific tasks.

TIP: Use the Right Tools
Ensure you have plenty of boxes, packing tape, labels, trash bags, and markers on hand. Consider renting or buying moving equipment like dollies or storage bins for heavy items. For shipping and storing, protect fragile items with bubble wrap, packing paper, or blankets. Have extra smaller containers at hand for sorting items like paperwork or trinkets. If you are packing stuff to sell in a sale (and not shipping it) remember you are packing it to survive a car ride, not for a trip around the world.

TIP: Use Technology

Technology is also a tool. Use it for the right situations. Digitize photos and memorabilia. Keep inventory of key items in Excel or other documents. Use a simple Project Charter for clarity and team communication. Photograph your progress if for no other reason than reminding yourself how much you've accomplished.

TIP: Respect the Emotional Aspect

Be patient. People may find it difficult to part with sentimental items. Offer gentle suggestions and allow time for them to process decisions. Keep a small box of sentimental items, making it easier to let go of other items.

TIP: Stay Organized

Document items for sale. If organizing an estate sale or donations, keep an inventory list for tracking.

Label everything. If not everything, as much as you can. Label boxes with both their contents and the room they are going to. For example, "Decorative Items, Living Room"

TIP: Don't Neglect Safety

Remind people to lift with their legs, not their back. Use proper equipment for moving heavy items. Ensure paths are clear for safe navigation and prevent tripping hazards during the sorting process. Wear gloves, masks, etc. for protection when dealing with potentially harmful items. In extreme situations, you may need (moldy home, hoarder home), a Hazmat suit.

TIP: Dispose of Items Properly

So maybe this isn't a tip, it's more of a warning. If items can't be reused or sold, try to donate or recycle before resorting to the trash, but don't trash the hazardous items. Handle hazardous items carefully. Some items like old paint, mercury, chemicals, or batteries may require special disposal methods.

TIP: Pace Yourself, Take Breaks, and Stay Hydrated
Downsizing can be physically and mentally draining. Take short, regular breaks to prevent burnout. Stay hydrated. Remind the team (and yourself) to drink plenty of water throughout the day.

TIP: Beware of The Family/Friend Expert
Help is great. But be wary of family members or friends who are "experts" in selling or valuing items. Use your intuition to guide you...Is this person genuinely trying to help or take advantage?

TIP: Celebrate Progress
Acknowledge accomplishments! When a room is fully downsized, take a moment to appreciate the progress. It boosts morale and keeps the team motivated.

TIP: Don't Panic
When you are in the process of actually doing the work, it's easy for your mind to take off and start to panic.

"It's all too much, I can't do this, what was I thinking, I can't believe Joe isn't helping."

When panic does grab you (and it will), take a deep breath and clear your mind. Here's what to do when it happens: look at the space directly in front of you, it may be a drawer, it may be a closet. Pick one small spot to go through. For example, a single shelf in a closet of 6 shelves. And go tackle that one spot or area. Clean it, make it stuff free. What happens is your mind gets back to task, you see that you made progress (because you did!), and you'll find yourself calm but energized to tackle the area next to the one you did.

By following these tips, the downsizing process can go more smoothly, ensuring both the team and the family feel supported and organized throughout the project. Remember, it's just stuff, you'll get through it. But if you still are unsure what to do with specific items, here are a few more tips:

"What Do I Do With…"

Some items are harder to part with than others, but that doesn't mean they have to go straight to the trash. Here's a list of common items that can be tricky to dispose of. Some ideas on what to do with them:

Old Clothing and Soft Goods Donate gently-used items to thrift stores or charitable organizations. You can also repurpose items for cleaning rags or upcycle them into something new. Animal shelters are a good place to donate used blankets and towels.

Books Donate to libraries, schools, or community centers. If they're outdated, consider recycling them or giving them to a book exchange program. Just check to make sure they are not valuable (i.e. look for first editions or rare books). Some downsizing companies take books just for the value of the paper so if you want to donate books that might get read and not shredded, donate to a charity or library. For instance, we found a couple of local places that sell the books we donate.

Old Electronics (e.g., phones, TVs, computers) Take them to an e-waste recycling center. Some stores (like Best Buy) offer trade-in programs or recycling services for electronics. Some older electronics can be sold but don't expect much for them. We take old electronics to a local electronics recycling company.

Toxic Chemicals (mercury, cleaning supplies, paint, pesticides) Take these items to your town's hazardous waste day or pay for them to be properly disposed of. Latex paint can be dried (kitty litter, etc.) and thrown away in regular trash. Check with your local hazardous waste disposal site for proper disposal methods.

Medications Many pharmacies offer medication take-back programs. Alternatively, check with local law enforcement for proper disposal options. You can always use the hospice method of dumping them in a cloth or diaper and pouring water on them, wrap them up and throw them away, but don't tell anyone we told you how.

Furniture Donate to a local charity, sell it online, or take it to a furniture recycling facility (aka dump) if it's no longer usable.

Mattresses Many mattress retailers offer recycling or trade-in options. You can also check with local recycling centers. Some states have specific disposal rules for mattresses. We try to sell them in estate sales if they are in good shape, but to be honest most people don't want them.

Old Photographs Scan or digitize them for long-term storage. If you can't keep them, consider giving them to family members who might appreciate the memories. The reality is that most people will not want them. Don't get too upset, sit down and go through some of them, and you will see what we mean. We recommend shredding photographs, treat them like an item that has special disposal needs (e.g. flags, religious items). We shred a lot of photos to maintain our client's privacy.

Toys Donate gently-used toys to donation centers, local shelters, schools, or community centers. If they're broken, check with local recycling programs, but most likely they will have to be thrown away. We toss used puzzles. (Who wants to count puzzle pieces to be sure they're all there, or to get a puzzle with missing pieces?)

Expired Food Throw it out. Obvious right? Our recommendation is to do it quickly especially with the refrigerator items. It's nasty cleaning out a refrigerator with rotten food. That being said, many municipalities offer food waste recycling programs if you have canned or otherwise "non-perishable" items. Check with local food banks or shelters. If you are wondering why we put this in as a topic, we often work for people that want to donate all their cans of food they stored in their basement - even though they expired in the 90's!

Holiday Decorations Donate to thrift stores or check with local schools for craft projects. If they're too worn, recycle materials like paper or metal. In general, while we will sell many holiday items, for those houses with huge number of them, we'll sell some and donate the rest. You can't believe some of the holiday collections out there! (If you think you have a large collection, we're betting you don't.)

Small Sentimental Items (e.g., Gifts, Awards) Consider passing them on to family or friends who would appreciate them or store them in a memory box or capture in a photo. To be honest, most are tossed. We'll pull the name plate (for client protection) whenever possible and donate or dispose of the award.

Old Paperwork Shred any confidential documents. Recycle the rest. If you're unsure, consider scanning them for digital records but that's a lot of work. When in doubt, we shred, it reduces the worry. There are companies that will do bulk shredding for a reasonable price. If you are worried about privacy and security of your information this is the way to go.

Batteries Take them to a recycling center that accepts batteries. Many hardware stores have drop-off locations.

Outdated Appliances (e.g., Microwaves, Toasters) If they are still usable, donate them. If they are really old, we toss them. We don't want to be responsible for a fire. Bring them to a recycling center that accepts appliances.

Garden Tools Donate to community gardens or local schools. If they're in poor condition, look for a recycling center that accepts metal tools. Sell the good ones in a yard or estate sale. You won't get much but you won't have to donate or trash them. You can always recycle them for the metal.

Jewelry and Watches Sell valuable or stylish items to a jeweler or in an estate sale. We sell tons of costume jewelry in estate sales. For broken, out-of-style and non-valuable items, consider donating them to charities or reusing them in arts and crafts.

CDs, DVDs, Cassettes, and VHS Tapes Donate to libraries, sell, or recycle. Some stores and non-profits may take old media. For VHS and cassettes, dispose of the homemade ones if no one in the family wants them.

Sporting Goods (e.g., Tennis Rackets, Skis) Donate to local schools, sports programs, or charities. If they're no longer usable, check if they can be recycled. Some will need to be disposed of, but only if they are unusable.

Chapter 13
Downsizing To Go - The Move

There's more to moving than just packing and unpacking. When moving a senior, there are extra steps to consider. The typical scenario involves transitioning from a larger home to an independent or assisted living facility. Here are some key considerations when moving to a smaller home. As with downsizing, we've broken it down into phases. A downsizing move involves three key phases: Planning, Packing, and Unpacking. Each phase requires thoughtful preparation to ensure a smooth transition.

Planning

In most cases, a move is required to transition the family member(s) into senior housing. This often involves transporting furniture and other belongings. Here's what you'll need to set up a smooth move:

> **Hire movers** Depending on the distance and size of the move, you have options ranging from large national companies for cross-country moves to smaller local services. Always get multiple estimates. Provide movers with a clear idea of what they will be moving (e.g., number of boxes, furniture).

Consider alternatives For some situations, using PODs or a similar service may be ideal. These can be loaded, shipped, and unloaded at the new location by services like Caring Transitions.

Do space planning Ensure the furniture and belongings will fit in the new space. Use hand-drawn plans or online tools to map out layouts. Avoid taking oversized furniture or items that won't fit comfortably.

Prepare a timeline Set realistic dates for each phase of the move. Allow time for sorting, packing, and cleaning.

Packing

Proper packing ensures the move goes smoothly. Here's how to make the packing process efficient and stress-free:

Create an inventory Use the list created during the Sort & Organize phase to prioritize what will be moved. Update it with the number of boxes as you pack to help movers plan effectively.

Prioritize essentials Pack medications, important documents, and daily-use items separately, and clearly label them. Keep these items in a separate, easily accessible box. If it will be a long-distance move, ensure there's a backup supply of medication in case of delays.

Label boxes Clearly label all boxes with their contents and the intended room destination. Use color-coded labels to make unpacking easier.

Pack sentimental items carefully Use bubble wrap and sturdy boxes to protect fragile and sentimental items. Overpack if necessary to prevent damage.

Minimize clutter Pack only what's necessary for the smaller space to simplify unpacking and reduce effort.

Use quality packing supplies Invest in good packing materials, including sturdy boxes and reliable tape.

Pack at a comfortable pace Move at a pace that's comfortable for the senior. Take breaks and use the time to reminisce together.

Consider professional packers Professional packing services can be invaluable for fragile or bulky items, especially if the senior has physical limitations.

Unpacking

Setting up the new space is as important as the packing process. Here's how to unpack effectively:

Focus on essentials first Unpack medications, clothing, and daily-use items immediately to reduce stress.

Make the space familiar Set up sentimental and familiar items early to make the new place feel like home. Photos, blankets, and decor items can provide comfort.

Involve the senior Engage the senior in deciding where to place items, giving them control and comfort over their new environment.

Avoid overcrowding Work room by room to prevent clutter and overwhelming the space. Remove any excess items promptly.

Ensure safety Arrange furniture and belongings to ensure clear pathways and easy access to commonly used items to reduce fall risks.

Provide emotional support Be patient and supportive. Moving can be emotionally taxing, so allow time for adjustment.

Dispose of packing materials Remove boxes and packing materials as you unpack to keep the space tidy and organized.

Do a final walk-through Conduct a walk-through with the senior to familiarize them with their new home and ensure they are comfortable.

Final Thoughts

Moving is inherently chaotic and stressful, but careful planning, thoughtful packing, and organized unpacking can ease the process. By setting up the new space with care and attention to the senior's needs, you can help them transition smoothly and create a comfortable new home.

When we set up a new space for our clients, such as a move to an assisted living center, we aim to make the environment as comfortable and familiar as possible. This includes arranging the kitchen similarly to how they had it, hanging family photos, placing art on the walls, and ensuring everything works, such as the phone and TV. The goal is to reduce stress as much as possible during this challenging time.

Chapter 14
Organizing for the Long Haul

Establishing Family-Friendly Storage Solutions

Maybe you just helped your aunt downsize. Or you've just downsized your own stuff. Now the job becomes keeping it up and not letting things get out of control. Staying organized may seem like a challenge, but wouldn't it be nice to find that tape you need without spending an hour trying to find it?

Also, no matter how much beloved stuff you live with currently, it will eventually be something that someone else will have to deal with. That's the reality. So, what can you do now to make sure things don't pile up or become a burden for you or your loved ones later? In our business, we are always relieved when we walk into homes that are already decluttered and organized. They are much easier, and cheaper, to downsize; and much better and safer to live in.

Certainly, there are a huge number of great books out there on decluttering and organizing (including this one!) to help, but here are a few simple strategies we employ to help keep items in the home at a manageable, and useful, level:

Do Nothing–Leave It as Is Use this approach if you have recently cleaned up, downsized or organized. Or if you are not emotionally ready to dive into organizing or letting go just yet. If you decide on this direction, at the very least we recommend not acquiring more stuff!

Start Small, and Spruce Up Regularly Every week, pick one room, drawer, or shelf to focus on. Small steps are often less intimidating and can create a ripple effect throughout the house. You'll build momentum as you see the difference in that one space. Paperwork, magazines and newspapers, old mail, junk drawers are always good to start and will make a difference.

Organize Your Entire House or Property Of course if you've already gone through the steps in this book, you're all set. But if you downsized your aunt's house, and have now turned to your own, you know this is the big leap! Organizing everything may sound overwhelming, but it can also be freeing. Start with a plan, one room at a time, and work toward the goal of a clutter-free, organized home.

Setting Goals for Decluttering and Organizing

Why are you organizing? The reasons will change over the course of your life. Knowing your purpose at the moment helps you make decisions that align with your current and future goals. Some common reasons include:

Helping Your Family Organizing can ease the burden on family members later. When things are neat and in their place, it will be easier for everyone to know what's valuable and what's sentimental.

Making Important Items Easy to Find Clearly identify and store valuable or essential items so that family members can easily find what matters most.

Keeping Things Private Everyone has those personal or "secret" items they'd rather keep to themselves. Organizing helps you designate spots for these things.

Assigning Heirlooms If you have specific plans for items like Aunt Ethel's china, organizing can ensure they end up in the right hands.

Someone's Moving Back Home A cluttered hobby room may have to make way for an adult child who's going back to school, saving for their own home, or staying to help an elderly relative.

Handling the Tough-to-Organize Items

In our experience with estates, certain items are always challenging. Here's a look at a few categories and some tips to help with these "pain in the butt" items that can add up very quickly:

Family Photos and Mementos These are usually the most sentimental items. Consider creating dedicated memory boxes for family photos and small keepsakes, or digitize photos for easy sharing. A family member might even enjoy organizing or archiving these memories. Try to do this periodically, so the job stays manageable.

Paperwork Sort paperwork into categories like "keep," "shred," and "scan." Store important documents like birth certificates, wills, and titles in a fireproof safe or digital storage for added security. At the very least, have a bin where you can toss obvious "toss" items, like the ones that are labelled "current resident" when the mail comes in.

Large, Bulky, and Heavy Items Items like pianos, old furniture, or large appliances are often difficult to move and store. Consider if they have a place in your future, or see if family, friends, or local donation centers can use them. Getting rid of them is a pain. Usually someone ends up paying someone to take the item. But, since it will have to go someday, plan for the removal now if you can, and free up some space as well.

The Key to Staying Organized: Practical Storage Solutions

Start by grouping similar items together—books with books, toys with toys, etc. Once sorted, select storage solutions that suit both your space and your family's needs. Here are a few helpful storage ideas:

Clear Bins and Labels Label, label, label. See-through bins make it easy to find what you need at a glance. Labels also help other family members know where things belong.

Drawer Dividers Use these for organizing smaller items. They're perfect for kitchen utensils, office supplies, and bathroom drawers.

Vertical Space Don't forget walls and doors! Use hooks, shelves, and over-the-door organizers to maximize vertical storage.

The goal is to create an easy-to-maintain system. When it's easy to find what you need, clutter is less likely to return.

Implementing Systems to Maintain Order

Getting organized is a great first step, but maintaining that order is the real challenge. Here are some simple systems to help you stay on top of things:

Family "Clean-Up Time" Set aside 10-15 minutes each day for everyone to put items back where they belong. It's a quick habit that makes a big difference.

The "One In, One Out" Rule Whenever you bring a new item into the house, something else has to go. This rule keeps things balanced and prevents clutter from creeping back in.

Regular Decluttering Sessions Every few months, set aside a day for a quick sweep of the house. Sort items into "keep," "donate," and "toss" piles to avoid letting clutter pile up again. Just like brushing your teeth, doing it regularly keeps things manageable.

Living Simply: Joyfully or Grumpily?

With your home now organized, you're ready to enjoy the benefits of a simpler life. Remember, living simply doesn't mean living without, you will have enough stuff. It means keeping just enough to make you happy and comfortable. Focus on the essentials that truly bring joy to you and your family.

Let Go of Perfection Perfect isn't the goal. Instead, aim for a space where you feel comfortable. It's not about impressing others; it's about creating a home that works for you.

Choose Experiences Over Things Less clutter can mean more time and space for activities you love, whether that's family game nights, cooking together, or simply enjoying a peaceful, tidy space.

The goal of downsizing and organizing isn't just to clear out stuff, it's to make room for more joy and meaning in your life. It's to create a safer place to live. Many of our clients hire us to merely declutter, sort and organize because they are staying in their homes. Once we're done, they feel relieved, and much happier with an organized house.

By maintaining your de-cluttered, sorted and organized space, you make more room for living!

Enjoy and keep up the good work!

ORGANIZING FOR THE LONG HAUL

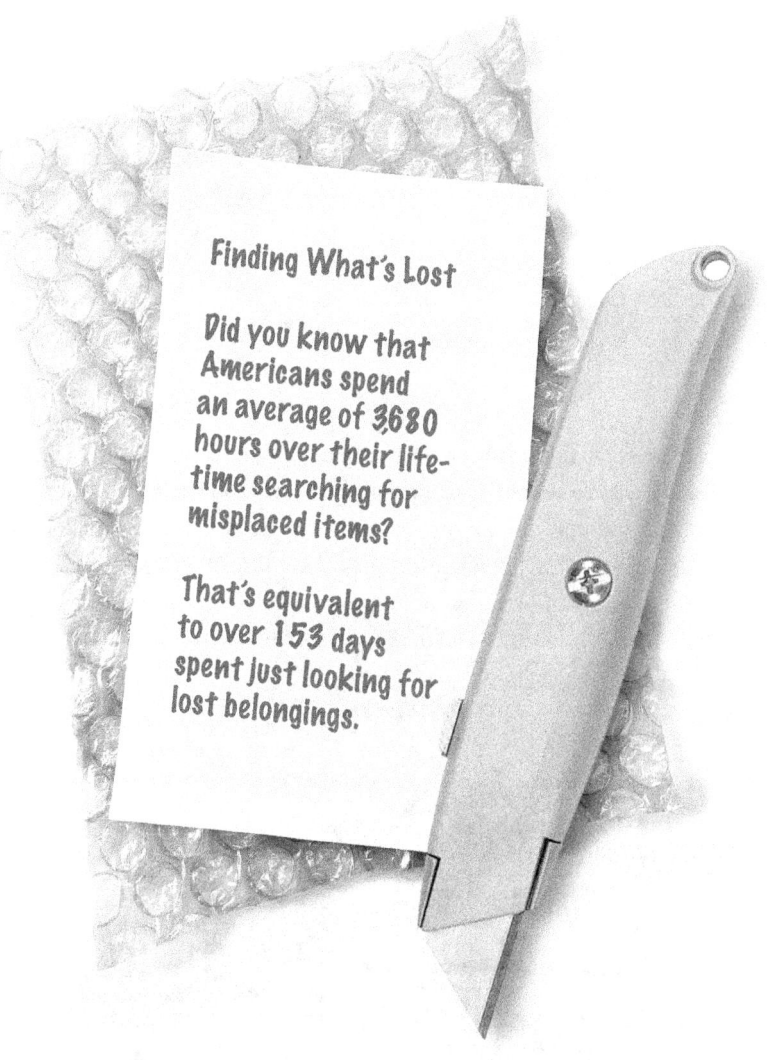

Finding What's Lost

Did you know that Americans spend an average of 3,680 hours over their lifetime searching for misplaced items?

That's equivalent to over 153 days spent just looking for lost belongings.

Chapter 15
Downsizing Hoarder Houses

We can't tell you how many of our prospects say something like "My uncle's house is a hoarder house!" or "I'm embarrassed for you to come in, I'm such a hoarder!" In most cases, it turns out to be an exaggeration. Their houses, like a lot of American houses, just contain a lot of stuff. Hoarder houses are on a different level. You'd know one when you see one, there's no mistaking a hoarder house.

How Do You Define a Hoarder House?

"A hoarder house is a residence that has become overwhelmingly cluttered due to excessive accumulation of items, often to the point where it affects the livability of the home. People who hoard typically have difficulty discarding possessions, even those of little or no value, which leads to extreme overcrowding. In a hoarder house, items may block pathways, cover furniture, and even create health and safety hazards, such as fire risks, pest infestations, or mold growth. The condition of a hoarder house can vary in severity, but it often requires extensive cleaning and organization to restore it to a functional state."

Well said, Google. That's it.

And we would add to that, "a common cause of hoarding is that we age; plain and simple. An illness or injury can put a family or loved one on the sidelines for a while. What doesn't stay on the sidelines is life, including trash, subscriptions, gifts bought from boredom, and other items that accumulate quicker than you might think. A cluttered home can quickly spiral into a hoarder house." While this may be an expanded view of the textbook definition of hoarding, we think it fits in the context of downsizing and gives it a little human perspective.

Most likely, your house is not really a hoarder house. It's got a ton of stuff in it, that's all, but if it is a hoarder house, how do you tackle the job? Or do you? Maybe not. When dealing with a hoarder house, deciding whether to handle the downsizing yourself or outsource to a professional company depends on several factors. Here are some reasons for each option:

Reasons to Downsize a Hoarder House Yourself:

Cost Savings Doing it yourself can save money, especially if you have the time and energy to invest in the project. Clearing hoarder houses is expensive because of safety issues and sheer volume of contents.

Family Heirlooms & Memories You may want to be closely involved in sorting through items, especially if they hold sentimental value or you need to make decisions on what stays and goes. You know there are family memories in there!

Privacy Some people may prefer to keep the process private, avoiding bringing strangers into the home. Some people are just embarrassed that their relatives lived the way they lived.

They collected items of value Hey, some hoarders have money and like to spend it on stuff they don't use.

Emotional Closure For some, personally sorting through the items may bring a sense of closure, especially if it's a family member's home.

Reasons to Outsource to a Professional Company:

Efficiency and Expertise Professional companies have experience handling hoarder houses and can work quickly and efficiently, knowing the best methods to clear clutter and handle tricky situations.

Safety Concerns Hoarder homes often present safety risks, such as structural damage, mold, pests, or sharp objects hidden in piles of clutter. A professional team will be equipped to handle these hazards. It's no fun having to clear a refrigerator that is full of months old food. It's gross, and nasty.

Emotional Distance Downsizing a hoarder house can be emotionally overwhelming, especially if you're connected to the person who lived there. Professionals provide a more objective approach and can make tough decisions more easily.

Physical Demands Hoarder homes often involve heavy lifting, sorting, and cleaning. If the physical demands are too much, a company can do the hard work for you.

Disposal and Donations Professional companies know where to take items for proper disposal, recycling, or donation, saving you the hassle of figuring out where things should go.

Legal and Environmental Compliance If the home has hazardous materials or sensitive items, professionals ensure everything is handled in compliance with local laws and environmental regulations.

Time Constraints If you need to clear out the house quickly (e.g., for a sale or move), professionals can speed up the process.

Two Types of Hoarder Houses and How to Approach Them

Dirty, Pest-Infested Hoarder Houses This house is full of rat-infested items, is dirty, and is not taken care of. There are usually some structural issues such as a rotten deck, leaking roof, broken windows, and other problems. The approach to these is a full cleanout with most of the items going into the dumpster.

"Clean" Hoarders Houses If the hoarder house is full of useful, quality items and the rodents haven't had a party in the house, then a big sorting and organizing effort is the key to start. It will be hard, but worth the effort.

Both types of hoarder houses present significant challenges, but each requires a different approach. If safety, efficiency, or emotional distance are a concern, outsourcing to a professional company is often the best choice. Here's an overview for each of the approaches.

Approach for Clearing a Rat-Infested Hoarder House - Low Value of Items

A rat-infested hoarder house poses serious health and safety risks, so the process must prioritize safety and sanitation. Since items often have little value in this case, the focus should be on efficient removal and disposal.

Step 1: Assess Safety Hazards

> **Professional Inspection** Before beginning, hire a professional to inspect the home for structural damage, electrical hazards, or other safety issues caused by the infestation.
>
> **Protective Gear** Ensure anyone entering the home wears proper protective gear, including masks, gloves, and sturdy footwear. This protects against exposure to bacteria, allergens, and rodent droppings. We use full suits with masks and head coverings (one-time-use paint suits work fine and are reasonably priced).
>
> **Pest Control** Call a pest control service to assess the infestation and eliminate the rats and other pests before beginning the cleanup.

Step 2: Prepare for Waste Removal

> **Dumpster Rental** Rent one or more large dumpsters for the removal of waste and damaged items. In severely infested homes, most belongings will probably need to be discarded due to contamination.
>
> **Trash Bags and Heavy-Duty Tool**s Bring heavy-duty trash bags, shovels, and large bins to remove waste. This allows you to work more efficiently in unsanitary conditions.

Step 3: Begin Large-Scale Disposal

> **Start in Open Areas** If there are any, that is! If not, start making your own space. Begin in high-traffic areas and focus on clearing

pathways. Remove all debris and damaged items from floors and surfaces. (We've had to shovel our way into the house, so sometimes you have to start clearing right inside the front door.)

Triage Belongings While most items may need to be discarded due to damage or contamination, evaluate large furniture or metal appliances that may be salvageable. Discard anything damaged beyond repair or clearly contaminated.

Step 4: Deep Clean the Space

Disinfect and Decontaminate After removing all items, deep clean and disinfect every surface. Pay special attention to areas affected by rodents and potential mold.

Final Pest Control Treatment Once cleared, schedule a follow-up pest control treatment to ensure the infestation doesn't return.

Step 5: Restore the Property

Repair and Renovate Once clean, assess the need for repairs or renovations, particularly if there was structural or electrical damage caused by pests.

Final Walkthrough Conduct a thorough walkthrough to ensure the home is cleared of all waste, safe, and ready for any future steps, such as selling or repurposing the property.

Approach for Clearing a Hoarder House with Valuable Items

When clearing a clean hoarder house that's packed with items, the focus shifts from sanitation to organization. In this case, many items may still hold value, so the process should prioritize sorting and finding a balance between what to keep, donate, sell, and discard. Follow the four-phase process to clear the house. We will point out some areas to focus on for hoarder houses.

Step 1: Make a Plan and Create Zones

Plan the Approach Set clear goals for the cleanup (e.g., downsizing, preparing for sale, making space). Determine if professional help is needed and gather necessary supplies (boxes, bins, labels).

Create Sorting Zones Designate areas for items to keep, donate, sell, and discard. You can create these sorting zones in each room or designate specific areas for each category.

The key to hoarder houses is making space as soon as possible. This is usually accomplished by removing high volume, low-value items such as papers, books, clothing. Remove obvious trash right away. If you have a question on an item, leave it or set it aside in the miscellaneous pile. That pile is bound to be very large for hoarder houses. Especially at the beginning of the process.

Step 2: Triage the Overall House, Then Room by Room

Categorize What They Hoard Are there themes such as antiques, books, trains, old cameras, etc.? Grouping similar items will help you decide what value there, how many duplicates there are, and how much time (and money) you are going to spend going through all that stuff.

Room-by-Room Approach Work systematically through each room, starting with the most cluttered areas. What are the themes of the room? That is, what are most of the contents of the room? There are usually themes, but not always.

Step 3: Follow phases 2–4 of the Downsizing Process.

Go through the Sort & Organize, Distribute and Fix & Final Cleanout phases. See Section 2 of this book to review.

Both approaches focus on safety, efficiency, and organization, but the rat-infested house requires more focus on sanitation, while the clean hoarder house emphasizes sorting and thoughtful decision-making.

Case Studies: The Case of the Hoarder Houses, Two Hoarder Houses, two solutions.

The "Dirty" House and Grandpa's Tools

The Client's Request
The client reached out with a rather heartfelt request, to locate his grandfather's cherished tools and items, believed to be somewhere in the home. These tools held sentimental value and were linked to memories of family craftsmanship.

The Situation:

This home was an example of the first type. It had been occupied by one of the daughters, who had taken control of the property under contentious family circumstances. Over time, she amassed a huge collection of items, from large purchases like RVs and boats to an overwhelming volume of QVC shopping hauls.

She lived in the Cape Cod home until her passing, which was a tragic and lonely end. She died on the front stairs, right inside the door, and wasn't found for two weeks. Sadly, her life as a hoarder had taken over every room. The smell upon entering, a combination of the decayed remnants of food, clutter, and death, was overpowering, making this what we call a "Vick's job," where you need Vicks VapoRub under your nose to mask the stench.

Our Approach:

Tackling this project was challenging. The client had tried on his own but wasn't able to get it done. Family members had abandoned attempts to help, too overwhelmed by the mess and emotional strain. Our team of three suited up for protection, ready for the physical and emotional toll that comes with cleaning a hoarder house.

We began by carving a path from the front door to the bedrooms and then to the basement, shoveling away layers of trash. Every move was an excavation, uncovering piles of canned goods, boxes, and endless papers. After days of work, we finally made headway to the basement, and the back shed, a chaotic jungle of overgrown bushes and brambles. Surprisingly, we found the RV pristine, a rare oasis of order amidst the chaos.

The Result:
Our persistence paid off. We uncovered his grandfather's tools, along with fishing gear and other keepsakes hidden amidst the clutter. The home eventually sold at a profit, and the grandson walked away with his grandfather's tools, a tangible link to his family heritage. The cleanout, while exhausting, had a rewarding ending for everyone involved.

House 2: The "Clean" House with Tasteful Overabundance

The Client's Background

Hoarding isn't always about necessity, it's often about boredom and convenience. For an older couple on Boston's north shore, years of online shopping filled the void of solitude and declining mobility, slowly transforming their home into a stockpile of eclectic items while their mobility decreased.

The Situation:

This house fit the second description, clean but overcrowded. An 1850s home, it had been expanded multiple times and was filled floor to ceiling. The husband had lived alone after his wife moved to assisted living. He passed away in the upper bedroom. Firefighters faced challenges extracting his body due to the overwhelming volume of accumulated items. They had to take him out of a window on the second floor.

When we were called in, we found not only the house filled but also three basement areas, a full POD, and an entire yard filled with everything from boats and canoes to a seven-foot anchor. The wife's health prevented her from handling the property, leaving the bank in charge and us with a unique challenge.

Our Approach:

Our first priority was safety. Our second priority was finding a list of family items scattered throughout the property. We carefully removed and cataloged 45 firearms and thousands of rounds of ammunition, followed by swords, knives, and other weapons. Only then could we begin cutting a path from the entryway to the living room, which had been buried under cigar boxes, clothes (many still in boxes), and assorted bric-à-brac. This room became our staging area, providing just enough space to sort through and organize items as we gradually cleared other areas.

The Result:

The firearms were sold to a gun dealer, cars to a car dealer, and boats were off-loaded along with maritime artifacts. Over the course of four estate sales and numerous donations (70 bags of clothing alone), we managed to empty the house and the cluttered yard with 4 30-yard dumpsters, plus tons of shred, donate, recycle, and hazardous waste. The project took over a year, with a six-month break for legal proceedings, but ultimately, the property was cleared and sold.

Chapter 16
Ways to Save Money in Downsizing

Clearing a home, or decluttering if someone is staying in it, can be costly. It is important to consider how well you want the job done and what the ultimate benefit will be (a quicker sale, for instance, or making a home more elder-friendly). Oftentimes, the choice of hiring someone to help comes down to getting the job done more quickly and efficiently.

Doing it yourself may seem like the cheapest option, but what will it really cost you in time and effort? Your time (and back!) have value too. When making these decisions, we encourage you to consider the potential ease and speed against hard work and time. That being said, we definitely have advice when it comes to saving during this process!

Plan Ahead

If possible, start the downsizing process before you have to. Talk to elderly parents and offer help to sort through papers and items in the attic and garage. You may even get some great stories out of it!

> **Shred** unnecessary paperwork like old receipts, bills, and outdated documents. Many people in older generations saved a lot of paperwork!

Donate or find a local reseller for shelves of unused books.

Decide whether to sell or donate bulky, unused furniture that won't fit in a smaller space.

Discuss with family whether certain items should be given to friends or relatives.

Starting early prevents rushing through decisions, which can lead to valuable items being lost or discarded during a last-minute move or sale.

Separate Personal and Family Items First

Whether you're handling the process yourself or hiring a service, this is a crucial first step. Professionals charge for the time they spend sorting photos, documents, and sentimental items, so doing this ahead of time saves money.

If relatives want certain items, like furniture or artwork, address this early. Waiting could add unnecessary service fees while items are held for decision-making. For families moving to assisted living, pre-select items to avoid accidental sales or donations.

Using a Hybrid Approach

Consider a mix of DIY efforts and professional help. For instance, handle the Sort & Organize phase yourself, then hire professionals for estate sales or cleanouts. Or do the cleanout after an estate sale is completed to save on additional costs.

Balancing time and money is key when deciding which tasks to outsource.

DIY Selling

As we mentioned before, platforms like Facebook Marketplace, Craigslist, and eBay are cost-effective for selling items directly. Keep in mind that items may sell quickly or take time, requiring your attention and effort. Garage and yard sales are excellent for clearing clutter but are best held after an estate sale to include leftover items. But don't expect people to pay much for the items.

Donate for Tax Deductions

Donating furniture, clothing, and household items can provide tax benefits. Always get a receipt for donations and consult with an estate attorney to confirm deductions.

Maximize Estate Sale Profits

To get the most out of an estate sale, separate family papers and personal items early, compare estate sale companies and their commission rates and resolve disputes over sale items beforehand to prevent delays.

DIY Moving and Cleanouts

Renting a truck and enlisting friends or family cuts moving costs. A pizza or two as payment often works wonders! For cleanouts, renting a dumpster may be more cost-effective than hiring a crew. Be cautious about tossing out valuable items during the process.

Use Outside Services Strategically

Hiring specific services for challenging tasks can save time and money:

> **Junk Removal** Condense items to reduce hauling costs and compare company rates.
>
> **Scrap Metal Removal** Many people will pick it up for free—never pay to remove scrap metal!

Re-Sellers and Donations Certain resale shops or donation centers may pick up large items for free.

Auction Houses Use auction services for high-value collectibles or artwork. Keep in mind they take a substantial commission.

Minimize Storage Costs

Storage units are an ongoing expense and often become long-term. Avoid this by being decisive about what to keep. If temporary storage is necessary, look for competitive rates or discounts. Long-term storage costs can add up to thousands of dollars over time.

Summary

Downsizing doesn't have to drain your wallet. By starting early, handling personal and family items first, and strategically using professional services, you can save both money and stress. Consider a hybrid approach and embrace DIY tasks when possible, but don't forget to factor in your time and energy. Avoid long-term storage costs by making clear decisions upfront. With careful planning and these tips, downsizing can be both economical and efficient.

Chapter 17
Murphy's Law of Downsizing

Downsizing by Murphy (and our team). This is stuff you can't make up. And it's true!

Murphy's Law of Downsizing

"The item you decide to throw or give away today will be the one you need tomorrow."
As soon as you get rid of it, you'll think you need it. Or worse, a family member will ask for it.

"The more you try to organize, the more disorganized it becomes."
Downsizing often creates temporary chaos before it gets clearer. Embrace the crazy.

"It will take twice as long–or more–than you think."
Downsizing always takes more time than you expect.

"The boxes you label "important" will be the ones that never get opened or get lost until next Christmas."
Somehow, the most critical boxes end up being the least used/needed. Still,

it's good to separate boxes, especially ones you'll need immediate access to. Have different color boxes, labels…and make the words large and visible.

"As soon as you donate something, you'll remember why you kept it."
Even if you do, it's okay that you let it go!

"The one person you expect to help, and need to help, will suddenly have other plans."
The more you count on someone, the more likely they'll suddenly become unavailable. It also can be really hard to get them to come back a second time.

"The piece you finally decided to sell will be the only thing that doesn't."
Estate sales love to challenge your expectations.

"Sentimental items take up more space than anything else."
Memories and keepsakes seem to multiply when you downsize. What are you going to do with 10,000 photos of mountains, anyway?

"Every room you clean will reveal at least three more rooms' worth of stuff."
It's as if items breed and multiply when you're not looking.

"You'll never have enough containers, boxes and bags until the end --when you have too many."
No matter how prepared you think you are, you'll need double the supplies.

"When you finally discovery the 'last key' in the house, a dozen more will pop up in the shed."
Keys multiply...It's a known phenomenon in the universe. Prepare to find your share when downsizing. No, they won't go to anything.

"At the estate sale, someone on your team will inevitably break the one knick-knack worth selling."
You think out of all those hundreds of knick-knacks, something may be of value. Nope, probably not.

"That box you saved for years will get thrown out the day before you find the item that fit ever so neatly in it."
Just throw out the damn boxes, it doesn't help value much by keeping the box. They take up need room in your house and in your mind. Get rid of them.

"The day you finally load up your rented truck/trailer overflowing with old furniture, garage and basement junk to dispose of, is the day the transfer station closes early because it's full."
Unfortunately, this one happens more times than you want.

"The item no one cared about for 20 years will spark a full-blown family argument the moment it's up for grabs."
Some family members just like to be difficult.

"The last thing left to move is always the biggest and heaviest piece on the property."
It's so easy to ignore, until you can't anymore.

"There will be at least three very important items lost during the downsizing project. These same items will be found later during the same downsizing project."
Things get moved around and moved around some more. Losing things, at least temporarily, is common. Don't panic.

These Murphy's Laws highlight the common frustrations people face when downsizing, but they also serve as a light-hearted reminder that it's all part of the process.

You're not alone!

Chapter 18
Putting It All Together

You may decide to use a service like ours when you choose to downsize a home. We have years of experience with all sorts of properties and bring a lot of that expertise (both emotional and practical) to the table. Whatever you decide, here are some more insights to help you come to a conclusion.

When we go through a property to review a potential job clearing contents, it doesn't take long to assess what's the best approach for the family. Why? As we go through the property we use our Four-Phase Process (see Section 2) to guide us.

We first assess the project, evaluate the home's contents, and determine what's valuable. We know that most of the items in the house can be easily distributed to their next home whether they are donated, sold, disposed of or recycled. Once we examine the contents, we can determine what the best approach for the family will be. For example:

Cleanout Plus Estate Sale This option makes sense if many items have resale value. This approach would also include disposing what remains after the sale.

Cleanout Only This would apply if there aren't many sellable items in the home.

Estate Sale and Partial Cleanout This may apply to a Downsizing To Stay scenario, where many of the home's items will remain, but a partial cleanout to make the property safter may be needed.

It's not an exact science to determine the best approach but if there aren't a lot of interesting and valuable items (see the chapter on what's valuable) then it probably doesn't make a lot of sense in trying to sell things. It's better to donate and cleanout.

Here's a quick recap of the important steps to help you and your family downsize successfully.

Focus on Family Items First When you start downsizing, begin with items that hold meaning for your family. Heirlooms, keepsakes, and sentimental pieces should be carefully sorted through first. Talk with family members to see what they want to keep. This could include things like jewelry, photo albums, or special furniture passed down through generations. Giving family members a chance to claim these items first helps honor your family's history and memories. Don't be surprised if the family doesn't want your china, china cabinets, or knick-knacks. If they want something they will ask. Don't be surprised if the only thing they want is some useful items. Remember to have someone in the family in charge to make the key decisions.

Heirlooms and Valuables Once you've taken care of family items, you can focus on other valuable pieces in the house. These might be antiques, art, or high-end furniture. For items that are valuable but not meaningful to the family, consider selling them. While an estate sale can help you sell most of your things, some higher-end items might do better if sold through other channels. Online auction sites or specialty shops can help you get a fair price for more expensive items.

Hold an Estate Sale if Necessary An estate sale is a great way to sell the majority of items that aren't staying in the family. You can have a company organize and run the sale for you, which takes some of the pressure off. Items like furniture, kitchenware, and decorations can find new homes while earning you some money in the process.

Sell Certain High-End Items Separately While some high-end items can attract estate sale buyers, others (e.g., diamond necklaces, high-end furniture) are better sold individually. For any items that have significant value—like rare collectibles, luxury goods, or high-end electronics—it's best to sell them separately from the estate sale or use them in the estate sale to attract buyers. Get a reduced commission on the high value items if you can. You can list them on online marketplaces, use auction sites, or even reach out to consignment shops. Find a dealer to buy them. This gives you the best chance of getting the right buyer and a better price. It just takes longer and isn't always successful. You can always put a reserve (aka 'a price') on expensive items (i.e. value over $500).

Donate or Discard the Rest Once the family has taken their meaningful items and you've sold the valuables, it's time to deal with what's left. Many things can be donated to local charities or thrift stores. If some items are no longer useful, it's okay to recycle or discard them.

Prepare the House for the Next Phase Whether the home is totally cleaned out and repaired or merely adapted with safety features to be senior-friendly, get the home ready for its new life.

Guiding Principles for Your Downsizing Efforts

Communicate throughout the process with the family team. We suggest, at a minimum, an email after the Plan phase is complete to summarize the team and goals. An email after the Sort & Organize phase, and a final email before completion. There are usually some last-minute items to complete. Remind yourself:

Don't sweat the small stuff It's just stuff, family is more important (even if you're not on the best of terms). If two people are fighting over an item, have them share it. They can figure out how to get the china cabinet from one house to the other!

Be Kind Throughout the Process Keeping things in perspective: this too shall pass. It helps in making the right decisions.

Embrace imperfection Yes, mistakes will be made. Just make sure the Ming Dynasty vase is safe!

Prioritize sentiment over stuff Determine what's really important (Remember, that will depend on the person)

Get help Embrace assistance from family, friends or someone you hire.

You don't have to get rid of your entire collection of things, just some or most of them. Remember to make a plan whether it's formal or informal. Think it through using this book as a guideline.

Please remember that the overall goal is to make it out alive (or at least without any major family problems!) Following the Four-Phase Process will give you the best chance to win in the game of downsizing. Luckily, unless you are crazy like us and love doing this for a living, you won't have to downsize many estates!

Finally, at the end of your downsizing efforts how will you know you have succeeded? Here's a checklist of success in downsizing:

Everyone is still talking to each other There is no new family drama. Less, actually.

The place looks good! The property is cleared or downsized as you planned it without too much added costs or stress.

No, or few, "oopses" Mistakes, broken, inadvertently thrown-away items have been kept to a minimum.

You feel more relaxed Your blood pressure is back to normal.

You've learned a lot Now your family and friends can go on and help another family downsize. Hey, they are pros now!

Everyone feels heard and respected All family members, even the obnoxious ones, feel like their opinions were considered, and they were involved in the decision-making process. Communication has been the key.

No storage units filled with stuff If you've achieved this goal, you win an extra gold star. But we know it's a tough one, so don't feel bad if this item isn't on your list of accomplishments.

Heirlooms/sentimental items are in the right hands Family heirlooms or sentimental pieces have been successfully distributed to family or friends who value them.

Charitable donations have been made Items you no longer needed went to charity, and you feel good knowing they'll help others, because they will.

You did good for the world You recycled and properly disposed of all the items in the estate.

A sense of accomplishment You feel proud of the work you and the team did. It wasn't always easy. Great job!

Downsizing is all about taking it step by step and focusing on what's most important to you and your family. Sometimes it's clearing out an entire property, sometimes it's just doing some downsizing to stay. Either way, by following our Process you can complete a job that to some seems impossible, but to you, will be quite manageable. You can do it.

In a way that doesn't stress you and your family out. We wish you the best of luck!

And always keep in mind: It's only stuff.

Appendix

Common Downsizing Situations and How to Approach Them

Over 55 Living

The Situation Downsizing can be overwhelming at any age, but in over-55 communities, it's often more manageable. These homes usually lack basements or attics, sparing residents from the accumulated burdens of generations. That said, the remaining items often carry sentimental or functional value, requiring a careful approach.

The Approach Homeowners moving into over-55 communities have usually undergone at least one downsizing move, so while the rooms are full, there's a sense of organization. Here, we focus on sifting through items that truly matter, ensuring family heirlooms and valuables are carefully documented. For most of these homes, the main challenge is the sheer volume of "brown furniture" and well-loved knickknacks, filling each room to near capacity.

The Result Once the main family items and valuables are set aside, the rest of the process moves quickly. The limited size of over-55 homes makes these jobs more straightforward, allowing us to move swiftly while preserving family memories.

The Collector

The Situation Collectors can present a different kind of challenge. In this case, a couple from Massachusetts had accumulated a massive collection of Byers Carolers and model trains over decades. Their 2,500-square-foot home had become a showcase of their passion, but as they prepared to transition to assisted living, they were faced with the need to pare down.

The Approach With collections as extensive and specific as these, it's often best to separate sales by category. We organized three distinct estate sales—one for Christmas items, one for the train collection, and one for household items. This allowed us to reach the right buyers and maximize the value for each type of collectible.

The Result All three sales were successful, covering the cleanout and move expenses. The couple moved to their new home with cherished memories and the essentials, while their beloved collections found new homes.

The Storage Unit

The Situation Storage units are a booming business because people accumulate more than their homes can hold. Often, these units hold a mixture of forgotten treasures and neglected junk.

The Approach Each unit requires a methodical approach. First, sort and organize to determine what's worth keeping. Then, we look for valuable items, anything from gold jewelry to rare memorabilia that might surprise even the original owner.

The Result Whether a unit holds priceless family heirlooms or miscellaneous items, the key is careful assessment. Every so often, we strike gold, literally and figuratively, making each storage unit an adventure in discovery.

The Cottage or Cabin

The Situation What type of cabin/cottage and the amount of time it's been sitting idle are both key in determining if you should just donate and trash most of the items.

> **The Approach** These structures are usually small enough that the family has picked the place clean so we come in, sort into our normal categories and go from there. Most times not a lot to sell.
>
> **The Result** It's usually a quick process that won't break the bank, but these are the types of jobs that some strong family members and a dumpster would do the trick, but there still is a lot to do so make sure you have the right resources to do everything, because as you know, everything is what we need in downsizing to go..

The Interloper

The Situation Somebody, whether it's a relative, friend, or tenant, is living in the house. The house needs to be emptied out and sold.

> **The Approach** These situations require some work to do a quick sort and organize to isolate the valuables and find family items in the initial sweep. It's not that people are thieves, no, not all of them—it's just that they "borrow" things for indefinite periods. Once word gets out that the house will be cleaned out, things start vanishing. So it's best to either jump in quickly to secure anything valuable or, better yet, let the interloper "help" clean it out, like raccoons at a trash can buffet.
>
> The trick is to balance tact and timing: be too slow, and you'll be saying

goodbye to the good silver; be too early, and you risk creating tension. Sometimes, setting firm boundaries with a friendly smile does the trick, but only if you're prepared to follow up.

The Result We've seen it go both ways. Some tenants or relatives turn into enthusiastic helpers, making the process smoother (and occasionally even finding forgotten treasures). But we've also seen the opposite, help that takes what they want or who declare *"I haven't seen it."*

With a bit of planning, patience, and good humor, you'll manage the interlopers and keep things (mostly) in place. Just don't be surprised if a few items find new homes along the way.

The Multi-Family Situation

The Situation When multiple family members have lived in the house or inherited it, things can get complicated. The house needs to be cleared out and possibly sold, but with several parties involved, everyone has different ideas about what should stay, what should go, and who gets what.

The Approach The key in these situations is clear planning and communication. Follow the Process and keep all parties informed. Be clear, it's the best way to handle the multi personalities and challenges. Make sure everyone knows their role.

The Result Sometimes, families pull together beautifully, each member respectfully picking a few sentimental items and happily letting the rest go. Other times, it's a free-for-all, with folks acting like they're on a shopping spree at a fire sale.

With patience and structure, the process can go smoothly, but be prepared for a few unexpected squabbles over old furniture or dusty knickknacks, but having a plan and communicating it is key to success in these efforts.

Divorce/Separation

The Situation A recently separated couple needs to clear out the home they once shared, whether to sell or split items as they move on to separate lives. Emotions may be high, and each party often has their own ideas about what's "theirs."

Never a fun situation for downsizing but the key to this one is good documentation, having a plan, and communicating (a common thread in all downsizing projects).

The Approach In these situations, diplomacy is key. Start with a joint list, identifying who values what and where there's agreement on dividing items. For some couples, this is relatively straightforward; for others, it's as tense as a standoff. Using an objective, step-by-step process can help defuse heated moments.

Focus first on the basics: sort out personal belongings, valuables, and essentials, and leave anything sentimental for later. If possible, have both parties agree on a "no drama" rule—and if that fails, sometimes it's best to bring in a neutral third party to keep things moving along.

Remember, it's a bit like separating ingredients in a recipe you both cooked together, things can get messy, but with care, it's manageable.

The Result Some couples are ready to move on and make it easy, working together like pros to divide things fairly. Other times, you'll see some emotional tug-of-war, with items mysteriously "claimed" or some last-minute changes.

With the right approach, though, most couples find a way to part peacefully (or at least without breaking any dishes). Stick to what's legal, plan and communicate so all parties are in agreement with the process and how items will be distributed.

Potential Companies To Assist With Your Downsizing:

Here's a detailed look at each type of vendor you might use during downsizing, including the types of companies available for each service:

Real Estate Agents
- **Mom-and-Pop Agencies** Often have deep local knowledge and personalized service. They may be better suited for unique properties or specific regional markets.
- **Franchise Real Estate Offices** Examples include RE/MAX, Century 21, and Keller Williams. These companies combine local expertise with a broader network and resources.
- **National Agencies** Companies like Redfin or Zillow offer robust online tools, which can appeal to tech-savvy sellers. They may be faster for simple listings but sometimes lack the local personal touch.

Estate Sale Organizers
- **Small Local Companies** Tend to know the community well and maybe be more hands-on, often customizing sales for local tastes.
- **Franchise-Based Estate Sale Companies** like Caring Transitions (franchise) offer consistent processes and access to larger advertising networks, which can attract more buyers.
- **Large Auction/Estate Sale Companies** Online-based auctioneers focus on a national market. They might be better for valuable or unique items that could attract out-of-town buyers.

Appraisers
- **Independent Local Appraisers** Often have specialized expertise in art, antiques, or collectibles. They're usually well-connected with local buyers and sellers.
- **Franchise or National Appraisal Companies** Examples include Sotheby's or Bonhams. While these companies offer significant expertise, they might primarily work with high-end items.

• **Online Valuation Services** Websites like Dr.Lori provide remote appraisals (they do much more and are amazing), useful for detailed assessments when a physical inspection isn't possible.

Auction Houses
• **Small Local Auction Houses** Familiar with local tastes and sometimes offer better commission rates. Good for mid-range items with local appeal.
• **Regional Auction Houses** Often hold both in-person and online auctions, expanding their reach. Examples include Doyle or Freeman's.
• **Large/National Auction Houses** Sotheby's, Christie's, and Heritage Auctions specialize in high-value collectibles and fine art. These firms often attract a global clientele for high-end sales.

Charity Pickup Services
• **Local Charities** Organizations like local churches or community centers often run donation pickups, and the proceeds directly benefit the community.
• **National Charities with Regional Branches** Goodwill, Habitat for Humanity, and Salvation Army offer well-established donation programs with some free pickup services.
• **Private Charity Haulers** Some smaller companies operate specifically to collect and distribute items to needy individuals or families, though these may charge a small fee.

Waste Disposal Services
• **Independent Junk Removal Services (aka the junk guy)** Often affordable and flexible, many local companies have fewer restrictions on the types of items they'll take.
• **Franchise-Based Companies** Examples include 1-800-GOT-JUNK? and College Hunks Hauling Junk. These companies usually offer easy scheduling, standardized pricing, and reliable service.
• **Municipal Services or Large National Chains** Some cities provide waste disposal services for large loads, while chains like Waste Management offer roll-off dumpsters for prolonged cleanouts.

Moving Companies
- **Small Local Movers** These companies are typically more affordable, may offer flexible options, and are especially useful for short-distance moves.
- **Franchise Moving Services** Companies like Two Men and a Truck or North American Van Lines specialize in regional moves, often providing packing services as well.
- **National Moving Companies** Large firms like United Van Lines or Allied handle complex moves, including long-distance, with extra services like storage-in-transit and vehicle transportation.

Storage Facility
- **Local Storage Providers** Often family-owned, these facilities may offer competitive pricing and personalized service but might lack modern amenities.
- **Franchise Storage Facilities** U-Haul, CubeSmart, and Life Storage have standardized pricing, secure facilities, and amenities like climate control, which are good for longer storage needs.
- **Portable Storage Services** PODS and 1-800-PACK-RAT offer portable containers, which can be delivered to the home for convenient packing and storage.

Cleaning Service
- **Independent Local Cleaners** Provide tailored service and tend to be flexible. They may offer more affordable rates and be willing to customize the cleaning process.
- **Franchise Cleaning Companies** Companies like Merry Maids and Molly Maid provide consistent service, pricing, and availability for deep or "move-out" cleanings.
- **Specialty Cleaning Companies** For more thorough cleaning, particularly if the property has unique needs (such as mold remediation), national companies like ServPro offer specialized services.

Handyman/Repair Service
- **Local Handyman Services** Small teams or solo handymen offer affordable and flexible solutions for minor repairs and touch-ups.
- **Franchise Services** Companies like Mr. Handyman or Ace Handyman Services have a network of skilled technicians and standardized pricing.
- **Specialized Repair Companies** Larger contractors or specialized repair firms handle more extensive repairs (e.g., roofing, plumbing) and are typically used if significant updates are needed.

Senior or Universal Design Consultant
- **Independent Local Consultants** Offer highly personalized services that can work with existing house for the best safety solution.
- **Franchises** Companies like TruBlue provide design and construction service for seniors.

Home Watch Service
- **Small Local Home Watch Companies** These businesses offer highly personalized services and may know the area well, providing in-depth property checks and tailored reports.
- **Property Management Companies** Many property management companies provide home watch services.

Specialty Movers
- **Local Moving Companies** Handle all types of local moves for a reasonable fee.
- **Franchise Services with Specialty Move Options** Companies like Mayflower and Allied offer specific handling services for oversized or fragile items.
- **National Moving Firms with Specialty Divisions** Large companies like Gentle Giant have divisions specifically for items like art and collectibles, offering both moving and temporary storage.

Document Shredding Service
- **Independent Local Shredding Services** Offer mobile shredding trucks and on-site services, often with personalized schedules.
- **National Shredding Companies** Companies like Shred-it offers on-demand or scheduled shredding with strong security protocols for larger volumes. They are great for downsizing. Just pay for a large bin (like the ones the school maintenance guys use) and dump it all in. We use it for photos too.
- **Office Supply Stores with Shredding Services** Staples and Office Depot offer in-store shredding drop-off, which can be a convenient and affordable option for smaller shredding needs.

Each type of vendor plays a unique role, and selecting the right one based on budget, flexibility, and service level will be determined during the planning phase. The good news is you will not need all the vendors, the bad news is you will use quite a few. Many companies, like Caring Transitions, provide many of the services above and can manage as much of the downsizing effort as you need.

How To Dispose of Items Properly

Hazardous Materials
- **Paints and Paint Thinners** Oil-based paints and solvents should go to hazardous waste facilities.
- **Pesticides and Herbicides** Chemicals used for gardening and pest control should go to hazardous waste facilities.
- **Cleaning Products** Strong acids, bases, or bleach-based products should go to hazardous waste facilities.
- **Motor Oil and Antifreeze** Often found in garages; these should never be poured down drains or tossed in the trash but instead should go to hazardous waste facilities.
- **Batteries** Car batteries and rechargeable batteries contain toxic chemicals and should go to recycling centers.

Electronics (E-Waste)
- Old Computers, Monitors, and Laptops
- Mobile Phones and Tablets
- Televisions
- Printers and Scanners
- Cables and Chargers

Many of these can be recycled at e-waste collection centers.

Medications

Expired or unused prescription drugs should not be flushed down the toilet. Most pharmacies or local governments have disposal bins. When our mother died the hospice nurse took her pain medications, dumped them in a diaper, put water on them and threw it away. It did the job.

Sharps and Medical Waste

Needles, syringes, and other medical items must be placed in approved sharps containers and disposed of according to local health department guidelines.

Asbestos-Containing Materials

Found in older insulation, flooring, or siding. Professional removal and disposal are often required.

Bulbs and Lighting

Fluorescent Bulbs and CFLs: Contain mercury and must be handled through proper recycling channels.

Fire Extinguishers

Old or unused fire extinguishers may still be pressurized and must be disposed of at hazardous waste facilities.

APPENDIX

Gasoline and Fuel
Where: Most towns have a Household Hazardous Waste (HHW) collection day, or a local hazardous waste facility that accepts fuels.
Tip: Many propane tank suppliers (like Blue Rhino) offer exchange programs where you drop off your old tank and pick up a filled one.

Appliances with Refrigerants
Refrigerators, freezers, and air conditioners contain freon or other refrigerants that must be properly removed.
Where: Contact your municipal recycling center or local appliance dealer. Some utility companies offer rebate pickup programs when buying a new appliance.
Tip: Private junk removal services may charge extra for these, so check if your town offers a free pickup first. Many metal recycling places take appliances. You still have to get it there of course.

Mattresses:
Where: Many areas now require mattress recycling. Use a local recycling center or recycling services in your area. Some states consider it a speciality item which means it has to be handled differently, and cost more money. Mattresses are a pain, we try to sell or give away the good ones but many times it's tough.
Tip: Some towns offer curbside mattress pickup with proper scheduling.

Tires:
Where: Most tire dealers, auto shops, or town transfer stations accept old tires for a small fee.
Tip: Never leave them roadside—it's illegal and doing so will carry a fine in many areas.

Building Materials

Things like adhesives, roofing tar, and treated wood often can't go in your regular dumpster. They have to be disposed of as hazardous waste during a hazardous waste day or a separate trip to the hazardous waste recycling center.

Where: For leftover materials, check with your local dump or landfill. Some construction supply stores accept returns or donations if the product is still usable.

Tip: Habitat for Humanity's ReStore may accept unused or lightly used materials like tiles, fixtures, or cabinets—but not hazardous products.

Items with special considerations:

U.S. Flags

- The U.S. Flag Code specifies that old, torn, or worn-out flags should be retired with dignity, usually by burning.
- Local veterans' organizations, such as the American Legion or Veterans of Foreign Wars (VFW), often hold flag retirement ceremonies.
- Some Boy Scout troops also perform this service.

Other Flags

For other national flags or regional flags, check local customs. If no guidelines exist, retiring the flag respectfully (e.g., folding and burying or recycling fabric appropriately) is often acceptable.

Religious Items

- **Holy Books (e.g., Bible, Quran, Torah, etc.)** Many faiths recommend that damaged or no-longer-needed holy books be buried, burned respectfully, or donated.

Contact a local religious leader for advice on proper disposal.

- **Religious Icons, Statues, or Rosaries** These can often be donated to religious organizations, charities, or thrift stores if they are in good condition. If disposal is necessary, some traditions recommend burying the item or breaking it into pieces to ensure it is no longer viewed as sacred.
- **Prayer Rugs** If no longer usable, many suggest they be washed, folded, and respectfully buried.

Cultural Artifacts or Ceremonial Items

- **Native American Items** Contact a tribal office or cultural center for guidance.
- **Ceremonial Objects (e.g., incense burners, chalices)** If they cannot be donated, burying them is often an accepted practice.

Items with Sentimental or Ethical Concerns

- **Family Heirlooms** Consider passing them on to family members who might want them.
- **Photos of Deceased Loved Ones** If you do not wish to keep them, consider scanning them before disposal. Shredding or burning respectfully ensures privacy.
- **Trophies or Awards** Many trophy shops will recycle or repurpose them. Alternatively, remove identifying plaques before disposal.

Best Practices for Symbolic Items

- **Consult Experts or Leaders** When in doubt, reach out to religious or cultural experts for guidance.
- **Donate Before Disposing** Many organizations, schools, or charities can give these items a second life.
- **Treat with Dignity** Always handle items with respect, even if they are no longer needed.

www.ingramcontent.com/pod-product-compliance
Lightning Source LLC
Chambersburg PA
CBHW051946290426
44110CB00015B/2126